Pearls

with love,
Jill Roree

Also by Jill Loree

The *Real. Clear.* series offers a fresh approach to timeless spiritual teachings, conveying profound ideas by way of easier-to-read language.
It's the Guide's wisdom in Jill Loree's words.

HOLY MOLY | *Real. Clear.* (Book One)
The Story of Duality, Darkness and a Daring Rescue

FINDING GOLD | *Real. Clear.* (Book Two)
The Search for Our Own Precious Self

BIBLE ME THIS | *Real. Clear.* (Book Three)
Releasing the Riddles of Holy Scripture

THE PULL | *Real. Clear.* (Book Four)
Relationships & their Spiritual Significance

PEARLS | *Real. Clear.* (Book Five)
A Mind-Opening Collection of 17 Fresh Spiritual Teachings

GEMS | *Real. Clear.* (Book Six)
A Multifaceted Collection of 16 Clear Spiritual Teachings

BONES | *Real. Clear.* (Book Seven)
A Building-Block Collection of 19 Fundamental
Spiritual Teachings

The *Self. Help.* series offers a bird's-eye view of the Guide's teachings and how to apply them in working with others.

SPILLING THE SCRIPT | *Self. Help.* (Book One)
An Intense Guide to Self-Knowing

HEALING THE HURT | *Self. Help.* (Book Two)
How to Help Using Spiritual Guidance

PITHY CAKES
Quippy Confections About Making it Through

www.phoenesse.com

The Guide Speaks website delivers spiritual truths by way of thousands of questions posed to the Guide and answered with candor and insight.

THE GUIDE SPEAKS
The Complete Q&A Collection
By Eva Pierrakos
with Jill Loree

www.theguidespeaks.org

Pearls

A Mind-Opening Collection of 17 Fresh Spiritual Teachings

Jill Loree

Real. Clear. | Book Five

Published by Phoenesse LLC
Discover more from Jill Loree at www.phoenesse.com.

ISBN-10: 1530265878
ISBN-13: 978-1530265879

Foreword

I am madly in love with this collection of teachings. Diving into each one illuminated a rich and important aspect of the Guide's message, until it came together in the end—a gorgeous string of wisdom. I don't claim to be the author of this grouping, but rather the receiver of the selected titles and the creator of a fresh new way to express the timeless beauty embodied in each. I have delighted in the co-creative process that I have been so fortunate to participate in. People, you are in for such a treat.

For anyone not familiar with these teachings, there isn't much you need to know. Each is self-evident and yet they build on each other and interconnect. The full body of roughly 250 teachings from the Guide is available online for free, in audio or written form. You'll find a link to each original lecture at the end of each chapter, or you can go directly to **www.pathwork.org**. You can also find a complete list of all the lectures at **www.phoenesse.com**, along with more of my freshened up collections.

Let yourself be immersed in these profound and practical creations, and like a glorious pearl, may the light then be reflected in all you do.

—Jill Loree

PEARLS

Contents

PEARLS

1

Privacy & Secrecy: A Boost or Bust
for Finding Closeness

Much as we may struggle to admit it, we all have needs: real, legitimate, have-a-right-to-have-them needs. One of these needs is for intimacy, for closeness. Another need, it turns out, is to have privacy. It's not hard to imagine that these two can be tricky to weave together. The fly in the ointment lies in our confusion between privacy and secrecy. Because when the two concepts of privacy and secrecy get cross-wired, closeness and intimacy become impossible.

Privacy, then, is not a nice-to-have, but a need-to-have. We need to have some time to be by and with ourselves. We need some me-time to dive into the depths of our interior, without being disturbed by even the most favorable vibes from our pals. Beyond this, sometimes we need some space to allow something we essentially desire to share with our loved ones to ripen, whether it's an artistic creation or a new insight or awareness. Some stuff just needs a chance to complete itself before we open it up to others. Hence, having some privacy is a legitimate soul need.

The periods of privacy we're talking about here are not the same as isolating or staying separate. In this case, a state of aloneness is a necessary means for finding more of ourselves. But of course, we all have a knack for also distorting any divine quality into its diabolical counterpart. And that's what happens when we seek privacy in order to avoid the anxiety created by contact. At that point, we've waded into distortion doo-doo.

Many of us completely miss this point that we have a need for some privacy. Being oblivious to this reality, we may find ourselves alone—perhaps through circumstances beyond our control—and then immediately set about cluttering up our inner landscape with noise. Surface thoughts, loud music, perpetual input—all these effectively avoid the deep inner contact our souls are craving. This can be one reason people gravitate to living in crowded conditions: they're producing an outer reason to avoid inner aloneness. Other people living in such conditions may manage to find their happy place despite the busyness that surrounds them.

Oddly, when people keep to themselves out of fear of contact with others, they are really primarily afraid of themselves; fear of self is the primary fear, followed by a fear of contact with others. Being alone then won't fill the bill of the need for privacy. In such cases, we don't come any closer to knowing or liking ourselves, just as we likely then won't forge true intimacy or contact with others when we take the opportunity to spend time with them.

So where does secrecy come in? First, let's be clear that the kind of secret we're talking about here is different from when we keep a lovely surprise party under wraps. In that case, we're planning all along to joyfully reveal the "secret." No, real secrets are never good because they are always hiding something negative. Otherwise they wouldn't be kept secret. The most surprising thing about secrets is the way we like to overlook this important fact.

Take apart any secret and we'll find the wish to hide something that we think will be unpalatable to someone. Either we want to keep something in hiding ourselves, or someone else wants us to help them keep something destructive hidden.

If we would reveal our secrets, we could deal with them. They could be dissolved and replaced with beautiful, positive creations. But when we keep things secret, we incubate our negative thoughts, nurture dishonest behaviors and sustain destructive ways of behaving.

And it's not like we don't know what we're doing. We're perfectly well aware of our charades and shenanigans—otherwise, once again, we wouldn't be keeping them a secret. To get all self-righteous about our bad behavior is really absurd. But that's about the time we trot out our "need for privacy," using it as a camouflage for our real intention, which is to keep things covered up in secrets. This is what secretive people do. And that's how the forces of darkness worm their way into our living rooms, banking on our confusion and handing us a truth to use in covering up a lie. They're good at what they do, and too often we fall for it.

Nothing that is true and beautiful ever needs to be kept a secret. Not ever. So something that is divinely inspired will ripen in privacy and then unfold when the time is right—it's never meant to be kept hidden. Secrets, on the other hand, are just the opposite, where we feel a need to hide our lies, dishonesty and destructiveness from others.

We may rationalize our secrets by saying, "If I reveal myself, I won't be understood," or "People will criticize me unfairly." But that's really taking things out of bounds. Because in truth, when we're in truth, we won't let possible misunderstandings from others justify the erection of impenetrable walls of secrecy. No, when we're standing in truth—or attempting to get to the bottom of it—we'll make an effort to help others understand. Further, we can use their pushback or criticism as an excavating tool to dig more deeply into the reality of a situation we might otherwise keep secret.

What's happening when we keep secrets is that we fear we're not in truth. Better yet, we often know we're not but we have no intention of changing. So then we're really being dishonest, since we know that others wouldn't react kindly to seeing what is hidden. And that's what we are try-ing to avoid. So we want their love and respect, but we have a sneaking suspicion we won't be able to earn it if they see what's behind the curtain.

In the final analysis then, keeping secrets is akin to theft. We're cheat-ing as a way to secure a result that won't come if we disclose our secret. And hey, we also sort of like the way it keeps things lopsided. We don't have to work at finding equitable, honest solutions that allow others to par-ticipate in the party.

That's how secrets become such killjoys for relationships. And that's why secretive people are never emotionally fulfilled. We build walls of separation that are plastered over with secrets, and then wonder why we feel alone and so very misunderstood. Folks, we need to put two and two together. Usually, we make things add up worse by blaming others for the state we're in: "I'm so worried about their reaction, I have to keep things secret. *It's their fault.*" Nothing justifies bad behavior like good ol' blame. It doesn't occur to us to spill out all our secrets and make ourselves transparent. And of course, this isn't a quick fix or an easy thing to do. We need to bring all the patience, discernment and goodwill we can muster to this task.

Sometimes we're just afraid of exposing ourselves. Fear whispers in our ear, "If they see the real me, they won't love me." Such reasoning has one little problem: it blatantly ignores the facts. For starters, we might be assuming that love, respect and approval from others outweighs the importance of our own. So not true. What's more, we may fail to see how the courage and honesty required for transparency—no matter what shameful things we're sitting on and needing to reveal—create way more self-esteem than any secretiveness could ever dream of. And if we start to love ourselves, love from others will follow.

When we follow a spiritual path, we are on a direct mission to eliminate all our secrets. First up: stop hiding things from ourselves. We keep our conscious minds in the dark—a lot. We need to realize just how much material we're ignoring, sticking it away in our unconscious where it breeds and multiplies. Once we start to develop a habit of being more honest with ourselves, we'll naturally begin to drop the veils between ourselves and others. If we continue in this way, we'll find it's the only way to be. It's the way to fulfill our need for contact and to live without fear and anxiety hanging over our heads. Ah, the relief of living without shame and hiding, without pretenses and façades. That, my friends, is a headier stuff than any two-bit secret.

So when we find ourselves sitting with suspicious opinions or accusations about someone, we need to pause and notice how we want to secretly nurse them—or worse yet, share them with someone who will hold our secret with us. All this we need to bring into the open. Doing so shows that our desire to be in truth exceeds our negative thoughts. It will become an organic process on our spiritual path to always search for the particular truth of any situation, and this will always bring us peace—if we are committed to real, unifying truth above all else.

Wanting to keep our secrets alive, however, clearly indicates that we are not yet committed to the truth—including the truth that we get off on maintaining this kind of negativity. On top of this, we want to continue our evil ways precisely because we already know we're not in truth and we don't want to admit this. And don't be fooled by those making loud, public accusations as though this is an indication of their openness. Such displays may merely be acts of hostility and aggression covering up a motive to still harbor negative opinions.

It's also important to realize that when we hold negative things in secret, we also keep a lid on revealing the best in ourselves. The lid of secrecy is one-size-fits-all, so when it's on we begin to feel embarrassed about our best ourselves. Our dreams and innermost desires will feel shameful.

The belief that there is anything to hide is what rolls in a fog that eventually covers up our greatness. So inherently positive aspects become shrouded in negativity whenever we are clinging to secrecy. We may discover, once the fog lifts, that our talents and gifts are part of what is being hidden. Until then, they may feel unworthy simply because they are being hidden.

As we make our way along our spiritual path—regardless of which path we're on—we need to gather the courage to expose everything we've been hiding. We will never regret making this step. It will usher in the freedom of no longer pretending in any way, and the clarity that comes from this will bring us straight to self-esteem—oh right, that thing we were hoping to get through our hiding.

The real way to reveal ourselves is by following the will of God, and then we need to let go of the results. Any rules about revealing don't rest with how others will react. It's possible we'll find at first that our self-revealing brings on criticism and censure, more so than love and understanding. We need to practice, practice, practice. Because somehow we have may have revealed ourselves in a distorted way. We can also let our revealing mirror our messed-up patterns back to us. The reaction from others can give us valuable information for reconsidering those same aspects in ourselves, now that we can see them more clearly.

The false way to go about self-revealing is to childishly say, in the warped way of the Lower Self: "If I share my secrets with you, no matter how destructive they may be, I demand you approve of me. If you don't, I'll accuse you of letting me down, and I will use this as proof that it doesn't pay to be transparent." We need to be careful about giving ourselves credit for opening up if we're going to do it in such a way. We want to make sure we sincerely desire to be in truth and in alignment with God's will.

Whoa Nelly, isn't it possible that others will leverage our openness as a way to violate our privacy? Indeed, others may try to pry into our business based on their own negative motives, hoping to uncover something they can use against us to make themselves feel better—all in a desperate attempt to prop up their own flagging self-esteem. When we sense this is happening, we need to call on our own discernment and re-secure our borders. The tricky part is to distinguish actual prying from genuine concern when we're still in the business of keeping our own secrets. As long as we have a stake in hiding, our perceptions will be shaky at best.

Think of transparency as the new black; it's a habit that looks good on everyone. But we'll need some patience and perseverance to wear it well. And we'll need to devote ourselves to learning this fine art. Sure, we're going to be hesitant at first, but our inhibitions will evaporate the more we learn to express ourselves, conveying what at first we didn't think we could ever get across. It's like trying to tell someone a dream. At first it seems almost impossible, but as we get rolling, we find we can explain it quite adequately.

When left inside the four walls of our minds, our thoughts, attitudes and feelings seem so vague. We think they are so unexplainable we don't attempt to convey them. But once we gain a smidge of confidence that we can do this—we can articulate our experience, even if we can't capture every little nuance—we'll be surprised at how well we can make ourselves clear. If we're willing to open up, we can reach others who may have the same inner experience. And in that way, we can connect emotionally more quickly than we ever suspected.

The point is, communication is essential to self-revealing. If we want to be open, effort will be required. But the rewards are fantastic. That stuff that appeared embarrassing only seemed so because we didn't believe we could find the proper words. Try—the words will come. Discovering a new and wonderful way of expressing ourselves is a huge booster shot for our sense of adequacy. If we sincerely want to reveal ourselves, we need to open up our willingness to let God inspire us. Then the appropriate words will flow and the walls we have built around ourselves will disappear.

Living in complete openness is the goal for any relationship: intimate partnerships, friendships, business colleagues, and even relationships between countries. For the new man and new woman who enter into a more evolved way of being in relationship, they will no longer keep secrets. Such behavior is simply not compatible with the newly emerging way of consciously relating. Secrets will feel like the unbearably heavy burden they are. In fact, the more our consciousness is infused with the Christ spirit, the more quickly we will want to dissolve such a burden, in whatever is the most productive and creative way possible.

In addition to the outer secrets, we need to be on the lookout for the more subtle inner ones. This means we need to be willing to take a risk to lay everything on the table, without which the bliss of relationship can't materialize anyway. The problem is our false belief that we're not good enough. We have to keep challenging this, over and over, every time it surfaces. Each time, we take a little more risk, until everything is out in the open. Then ongoing communication can be established.

Like an engine in which gunk builds up over time, we're going to find some residual crud in the pipes. Once we clear out the sludge though, making all of ourselves known, a new process will automatically take over. Our souls are not fixed, static things; we're constantly changing and moving, producing new inner vistas and visions. With whistle-clean pipes, we'll be in good shape to share what emerges with our loved one. Such transparency then is our path to utter joy.

When it comes to our friendships, we don't do them justice if we feel there is anything we must keep hidden. For then we'll never know if we are loved and accepted. If we fail to take the risk of showing our friends all that we are—all that we have kept hidden—we'll remain in fear and distrust. We need to be willing to look at our Lower Self goals—which are always primarily to keep us in separation—and trust that our Higher Self aim for connection will carry us through. If trust is what we lack, we can start by sharing that.

Even the interactions between countries are often enormously impacted by secretiveness. To be sure, there is more hiding and pretense there than in any other relationship. Openness is often simply not considered a viable option for governments of different countries. Opaqueness, it is believed, makes for sound diplomacy.

In this area, humanity has fallen far off the pace of where we could and should be, although other areas also leave something to be desired. Consider how people in a marriage often keep secrets, not just about the past but also about present-day thoughts and feelings. Look at how this correlates to the failure of so many marriages. Yet most marriages are better off than the interrelationships between countries, which are often mired in distrust, strife and deceit. We need a whole new game plan if we're hoping for peace to break out around the world. Then we will be able to share God's riches. Otherwise justice and brotherhood will remain empty words.

Just as individuals need to go through the painstaking process of learning to be open, so must countries. But what's the alternative? We can't get to peace and harmony any other way. It's like trying to live life while projecting a false version of ourselves, basically saying, "Please see me only as I pretend to be." It's going to be hard to forge an authentic, trusting connection on top of that.

Can you visualize a world in which no one ever hides anything from anyone? Ever? Would that not be paradise? What stops us is 1) our fear of risking rejection if the other saw our real self (we are secretly terrified that our Lower Self makes us all bad), 2) our unfamiliarity with how to communicate so we are understood (we must be willing to learn to do this, baby step by baby step), and 3) our fear of being insanely invulnerable if all our hard shells fall off (secrets are among the hardest layers surrounding our souls).

What's the common denominator of these three factors? Our resistance to going to God with all of ourselves—to trusting his will. Instead, we let the dark forces grab us and inspire us to trust in whatever keeps us separate. We mistakenly think that's code for "safe." We've got to wake up and see that this is no way to live. We desperately need to start challenging this logic; we have to choose new behaviors and seek new solutions.

A few final thoughts about the third factor: vulnerability. There's more to this than feeling less protected without our secrets, which is in fact an out-and-out illusion—and actually an easy one to spot once we crank up the courage to get over ourselves. But there's also another kind of vulnerability.

We're going to find that as we open up, new capacities for perception will grow in us. We'll experience clarity about many areas of life that were vague and murky before. If we're not looking for this though, we'll miss it, because too much fog and darkness still cling to the edges of our reality.

But wait, there's more. At first blush, this one may not look like a winner. Our emerging sense of vulnerability may bring with it a grieving pain regarding the destruction that results from evil in our midst. It's OK to let this develop, to experience this fully, however it manifests. It's actually a healthy pain that arises when we see God's gifts squandered—when, for example, nature is willfully destroyed.

We may feel this pain about the suffering of animals who, as part of fulfilling their function in the greater life cycle, become prey for other animals. Certainly this is much less hurtful than the suffering inflicted on animals by indifferent or cruel humans, but nonetheless, it is painful that animals must go through this phase in their own evolution, even as there is an intrinsic rightness about this. These animals are aspects of consciousness which have incarnated to have these experiences, but there is an innocence there that causes us to feel pain for them.

So why must we open to feeling this kind of pain that arises from our compassion and gratitude for the beauty of creation? Because this soft pain—which is so different from our neurotic, self-punishing, victimy pain—is a threshold to feeling joy and ecstasy. It's by opening to this pain that we recognize that untrue thoughts about any of our fellow humans is as damaging to ourselves as it is to others. When we malign others or hold onto unwarranted suspicions, we impose unfair disadvantages on them. We make them our prey.

As long as we deny this pain, we pay a higher and higher price. For this pain must eventually turn against whoever is inflicting it—or against whoever colludes with others by passively standing by. We have to let ourselves know and feel this pain instead of following the dark forces into a blind alley where we pretend we don't see the pain we cause another. When we do that, debilitating guilt is sure to follow us and then self-punishment heaps onto that. Our compassion and willingness to simply see the pain that exists in this world will make us whole again.

Then, when the secrets and their walls of separation fall away, we can step into a beautiful world of light and goodness, of singing joy and fearless existence. Such a world can only exist in a defenseless person who has taken off their armor and no longer denies the soft underbelly of vulnerability. Hardening against the pain of all the suffering surrounding us—caused by our cooperation with the forces of evil—has the direct effect of blocking the joy that is meant to be ours for all of eternity.

If we are willing, we can harness the power of the forces of light and become an even stronger fighter for good. The blessings of all the angels accompanies each one of us, enriching and guiding our lives. The presence of Christ is alive in our hearts and souls, if we will only see and feel it. Our whole reason for being on this planet is to find our true being and fulfill ourselves through God. We can come alive through him.

#252 Privacy and Secrecy

2

Reading Between the Lines
of the Lord's Prayer

Nestled within the Lord's Prayer is everything we ever need; it contains it all. Here, then, are the Guide's teachings about how we can apply it in a personal way to solve any problem.

OUR FATHER

This short phrase may conjure up a picture of God as a literal father to humankind. So as we say these words softly inside ourselves, we can meditate on how this must apply to everyone, even those we don't happen to like. We can let the slideshow run of all those people we have some disharmony with, including those we full-on hate and those we just feel some minor resistance to or irritation with. Dropping into stillness, we can pause and consider that these people too are children of God.

In fact, we can only call ourselves children of God if we're willing to open the gates to all the creeps and crapheads in our world. Either no one's in this flock or everyone is, even those who bring up unpleasant feelings in us. Opening our arms this wide has the subtle effect of shifting our attitude and therefore our feelings, even if ever so slightly. We will become more free and relaxed.

Our first reaction to opening to inclusion may be resistance; our feelings aren't always so willing to change. In fact, holding onto strong negative feelings creates tight inner knots inside us, and they aren't so quick to let go. So consider any resistance to be red flags saying 'ding, ding, ding, there's a knot here waiting to be dissolved.' Important tip: try not to ignore red flags.

Whenever we have angst about another, there is something in us that needs attention, *no matter how wrong the other person may be.* This insight unlocks the latch on whatever we need to straighten out inside ourselves, making us ready for new recognitions, teachings or inspirations. Then real, practical means can show up to help us free ourselves from our stuck, stinking state.

Ask for it. Want it. And then all of a sudden, as we sit in meditation and deeply ponder these words and how we can apply them, a pressure will lift up off our chests. The lock will release and we will feel ourselves freed from a heavy burden.

Here's another way to work with this. We can skip over everything that bugs us about someone, and visualize how they are perfect. Where is that divine spark in them? How does it show itself? Never forget that all who seek will find. We can actively search for the qualities in them that stream from their Higher Self—the ones that qualify them to also be called children of God.

We have to learn to draw a line between Higher Self qualities and those coming from the Lower Self domain. We can pinpoint which comes from where. The Higher Self is eternal and immortal—it's of God. The Lower Self is temporary and based on illusion. Let's start by looking at the home team before we start sizing up others. Once we can distinguish both in ourselves, it won't be so hard to love our neighbor; it will become so much easier to recognize someone we don't like as our brother or sister. Then our own Higher Self can stream forth and connect with the Higher Self in the other. Namaste.

That's what's contained in the first two words of the Lord's Prayer.

WHO ART IN HEAVEN

Heaven is inside us, not outside. So we must look for what we're seeking—to find our own perfection—within, where it already exists. It may however be covered over and difficult to find. We must also seek heaven, which is the same as seeking God, inside the soul of our brothers and sisters—even of the ones we reject. That's where we can find the eternal, living God.

HALLOWED BE THY NAME

The way to hallow the name of God, the father, is to try to fathom his laws and follow them. And there are a bunch of spiritual laws—one for every aspect of life. Whenever we find ourselves stumped by any life situation, it means we haven't found the specific law we're violating.

So when we say we want to hallow thy name, we are really asking, "Where am I struggling? What are my problems? Somewhere I am not in keeping with a spiritual law, even if I'm not aware of it—and I don't want to do this any more. Show me."

By asking God to help us understand what spiritual law we are breaking, we learn to establish a personal connection with God, and in that way we truly hallow his name. For any time we are willing to be in truth about our problems, asking for help with an honest heart, we will get an answer. It may not come at exactly the same moment of our asking, but if we open our eyes and look, life will bring us answers.

THY KINGDOM COME

When we follow spiritual laws, hallowing God's name, we also bring ourselves closer to his kingdom. *Because it's within.* But if we had to think about where God's kingdom is, most of us would put it "somewhere out there." We think it's going to descend to Earth and all we'll have to do is go to where God's kingdom is and walk in. Many of us have this kind of vague made-up idea rolling around in our imaginations.

Our work, however, is to create God's kingdom within ourselves. And that can only happen when we successfully navigate our way through Earth school, learning about spiritual laws and applying them in the proper way.

THY WILL BE DONE

Simple but not easy, this one. We're the ones making it so hard. We go around claiming we don't know what God's will is, but for sure, if we knew it, we would totally follow it. We forget about that part where our prayers for assistance are never answered with a stone. So if we try to make contact with Spirit World of God, asking to know his will and desiring to fulfill it, we're going to get an answer. Even while we still have doubt. We don't need to rack our brains wondering 'what, oh what, would God have me do?' If we're unsure, we only need to turn to the areas where we don't yet need an answer. The answers will then become obvious, once we start to think.

Here's a no-brainer: God's will is for each one of us to follow a path—in whatever way it appears—toward purification of our souls. We can also bet on it being God's will that we face ourselves honestly, instead of doing what we usually do, which is to push away anything that makes us uneasy. Then we blame circumstances or other people, hoping to find a scapegoat so we won't have to look within for what's the matter.

Take any inner resistance, contemplate its cause for a moment, and Shazam, we can be sure to find that we have violated a divine law. No one else's wrongdoing or error of any kind has the power to make us feel disharmonious inside unless there's something amiss inside us as well. In the end, any of our inner feelings of disharmony—heaviness, anger, resistance, fear—signal that we have, in some way, failed to fulfill the will of God.

Something in us, then, doesn't square with the world. Otherwise, there wouldn't be so much darkness in some of our life situations. Again, if we wholeheartedly want to know what it's about and how to fulfill God's will, we only need to ask. The answer may take a while, but sooner or later it must come.

Don't be afraid. God's will is not something to fear. It's always wise and loving and leads us to happiness, even if this means struggling through a tricky transition. We can ask ourselves, "Am I ready to sign up for doing God's will, even if I'm not crazy about it at first?"

ON EARTH AS IT IS IN HEAVEN

OK, now what on Earth does this mean? Are we really praying that God's will be done in heaven—you know, that mysterious "somewhere" located somewhere "out there"? More than that, if such a place existed, would it need our prayers that God's will be done there? Do we think that, like, we would have some say in this? Certainly not.

In truth, we do have some say, to some degree, here on Earth, if we follow a spiritual path of self-development as a way to spread more light into the world, working on behalf of God's kingdom here on the home planet.

But keep in mind, heaven is within. That's where our spirit is hanging out in all it's original perfection, waiting for us to break through the walls of our Lower Self to find it. To what extent is this God within—the essence of who we are—already manifesting in our earthly reality? Where does God not yet shine through into our actions, our thoughts and our feelings? Try this on for size: where do we hold some tight conviction or opinion that we cling to, believing it is God's will? Would we be willing to loosen our death grip and let it go, considering the possibility that maybe it's not quite so? Or would we rather hang on, convincing ourselves it must be this way?

Really try to find an area in life where you cling to something. Now, be honest: is it more important to know the truth or cling to a tightly held conviction? If we're right, do we trust that we can let it go and God will confirm it? Any time we feel a tightening band of rigidity—regardless of whether our opinion is actually right—we prevent the heavenly kingdom from manifesting within. Of course, if we're in error, we're already blocking the truth and God's kingdom stays locked away.

GIVE US TODAY OUR DAILY BREAD

We tend to repeat this part like a mantra, without giving it too much thought. We assume, although often without clearly formulating the thought, that earning our keep doesn't have much to do with God. But truly, we can't do anything good if it's not blessed by God. Without his help and guidance, we're dead in the water, no matter how hard we try again and again.

If we've done even a little self-development work, we have enough awareness to reflect on our lives and see which parts had God's blessing and which did not. Feel the difference? How about looking at areas where we repeatedly fail—our trouble spots. What's the real reason for this? Where did we go wrong? Where is our attitude off base? These questions are good food for thought. Can we surrender ourselves entirely to God?

In saying this part of the Lord's Prayer, we are asking to be guided in obtaining both our earthly bread and our spiritual sustenance. Typically, our spiritual bread is terribly neglected; we think it matters so much less than our material bread. No, folks, it's the other way around. Our spiritual bread feeds our soul and is much, much, much more important. We need to want it—to desire to be spiritually nourished. This is the gateway through which all our earthly problems get resolved, and not vice versa. Once we start yearning for spiritual bread, we are making nice progress in moving along our spiritual path.

FORGIVE US OUR TRESPASSES

The operative word here is "us." We're asking God to *forgive us*, not me alone. That means everyone, including those who have hurt us and who we may still be struggling to forgive. If we can honestly wish that God forgives them, we free ourselves from a dark spiritual form inside us that attracts harmful energies and other dark influences. Wow, now that's really saying something.

So we're really asking that God forgive not only us and those we love, but also those against whom we still hold a grudge. That's what we're really guilty of and for which we can ask to be forgiven.

Let's talk about this guilt for a minute, because often we are not clear about our own actual guilt. Instead, we produce exaggerated feelings of guilt that are not justified; they are false and unhealthy. Here's how the inner process works. We don't want to admit to the areas where our guilt is justified, where a genuine, constructive repentance would go a long ways without dragging us down or discouraging us. We could ask God to forgive us, and if we really want to change, we will feel liberated by the forgiveness we receive. A burden will lift off our shoulders when we carry through with our sincere, good intentions.

But no, too often we won't face our real guilt. In our pride, we want to see ourselves as better than we are. Beyond this, we know that inner change isn't easy; it won't happen overnight and an effort will be required.

From the core of our being, signals arise that spur us to recognize our guilt—where we are in the wrong. But our Lower Self, with its pride and laziness, gets into the mix, so we adopt a guilt that isn't genuine. It's like we're saying, "You know, I'm really sorry about everything, but I'm not the one who's really guilty here." This hidden notion needs to be brought into the light of day. Seeing it will help move us from suffering false guilt to gaining real forgiveness.

Here's a nice bonus: once we recognize our real guilt, we automatically lose all false guilt complexes that pull us down; we will know peace. The struggle is in opening ourselves wide so we can overcome our own resistance. We're afraid to admit to our real guilt—where we have in some way hurt someone else—preferring instead to cover up our faults. In that moment, we want to be better than we are and can't accept that, right now, we're not very perfect. Facing our real guilt for this truth will lead to liberation; sitting with false guilt complexes will not. The truth might be a bitter pill to swallow, but that's our medicine that will help us heal. False guilt only leads to more of the same, with heaviness and sadness heaped on top.

We need to examine ourselves closely to see all this. It is only by penetrating all our layers of delusion that we find how we are responsible for causing pain. In our actions or emotions, we have violated some spiritual laws and we can ask God to forgive us; we can also ask to be shown the error of our ways and how to change. Only after we free ourselves in this way can we totally forgive another. Expecting forgiveness for ourselves, then, goes hand-and-hand with being ready to forgive. And then once we've experienced the balm of God's forgiveness, we will be able to forgive ourselves. This leads us to the next line in the prayer.

AS WE FORGIVE THOSE WHO TRESPASS AGAINST US

How many times have we said the Lord's Prayer knowing full well that we have no intention of forgiving someone? That's called self-deception, or aka, kidding ourselves. While we may be past the point of hate, resentment still smolders and until we're clear from that, we're not free enough to have spiritual experiences. We lack the ability to completely forgive because we lack the ability to understand the other person. This, though, we can pray for help with—to gain the insight we are lacking. As long as we really want it and are willing to stop wallowing in our resentments—which we like to do, *a lot*—then all this will be given to us.

The thing we are most thickheaded about understanding is that there are things we can't do by ourselves. Like forgive. We all need help on this one. That's why this phrase is included in the Lord's Prayer. If we could forgive all on our own using the power of our will alone, we wouldn't need to pray for help, would we? Like, for example, we don't need to ask for help moving from Point A to Point B because we have legs we can move at will. But forgiveness, that we need to ask for help with. That, and the ability to face ourselves in total honesty—to come to know ourselves without our masks. And to tackle our resistance and make real inner change. So we must pray.

Remember, not forgiving is a light-blocking burden that makes our heart unhappy. It harms us way more than it harms the one we won't forgive. We need to be willing to confront ourselves: "Do I really and truly forgive so-and-so from the bottom of my heart?" When we are able to see clearly that we can't yet quite get there alone, we can always ask for help.

LEAD US IN OUR TEMPTATIONS

Notice the nuance of the wording here. What we usually say is "Lead us not into temptation," which can easily create a harmful misconception. For God doesn't lead us into temptation. Rather, what this phrase means is that we should pray that God will lead us when we are feeling tempted. We pray that God guides us so we resist temptation, helping us have the fortitude to be victorious. Regardless which words we choose to say, it is important that we have a correct understanding about the concept.

So what exactly is temptation? To begin with, it's within us; it doesn't come to us from the outside. Even if it did, we wouldn't yield to it if it didn't have a matching receptor site inside us. We have to learn that we can be tempted, and in just what way. For instance, can we be tempted to commit murder? Of course not. But we can be tempted to give in to our own faults, whatever they are. *So we need to get to know our own faults.* We should list them out so we remember them and then pray for help in overcoming them. As with forgiveness, we can't tackle our faults all on our own. But notice how tempting it is to think we can—that we don't need any help.

Call it what we may—the devil, evil, Satan or bum luck—nothing bad can get at us unless we have something in us that responds. So it's an error to think that we can pray for God to keep bad things away. No, the germ of whatever tempts us lives in our own Lower Self, the crust that envelops our perfect inner self. The dark forces merely serve as instruments to draw it out. They bring our negativities right into our awareness where, if we want to, we can fight them. If that germ of evil remained dormant, with no chance of manifesting, we wouldn't come a single step closer to perfection and genuine bliss. (Did you just catch a glimpse of the genius of God's laws?)

BUT DELIVER US FROM EVIL

Same idea—the evil is in us. If it were only outside us, it couldn't touch us. We can drop this thought into our prayers, asking Christ to help us overcome temptations so that we can deliver ourselves from evil. We're the only ones who can do this—with the help of God and Christ, just as promised.

Try asking for help, but don't try going it alone. We aren't strong enough for that. Even with all our willpower and unceasing effort, we're as powerless as God—or Christ or any spirit helper—would be without our will to free ourselves. So both are needed: our willpower and the help of God. We need to come at things from both angles, doing our own work and also asking for spiritual help, over and over.

FOR THINE IS THE KINGDOM

God's kingdom is within. It belongs to God and no one else.

THE POWER

God's power makes us capable of love and understanding. It lifts the lid on the darkness and imperfection we have carried with us for so many lifetimes. It cleanses us and illuminates the truth, bringing us to the ultimate conclusion.

AND THE GLORY

This we can only attain by following God's will.

The Lord's Prayer is the most beautiful of all prayers because of the way it holds everything—yes, everything—we need to live a glorious life. So much more could be said, but we can also access further depths of meaning ourselves by making this a living prayer. Sit with each phrase and let the meaning of the words expand as further interpretations become more and more clear. Notice how the prayer already lives in some areas of your life but lies dormant in others. Bring it all to life.

If we live our lives this way, we must ultimately become happy and our problems will disappear. For now, our problems are our necessary medicine. Later, when we begin to master our lives, instead of the other way around, we will embody a happiness that can be shared with others. But if we're unhappy, we can't make others happy. This simple yardstick of 'how happy am I?' lets us measure how much happiness we are able to give. If we truly desire to make others happy, God will guide us in receiving the medicine that will allow us to heal, so it can be so, forever and ever. Amen.

#9 Prayer and Meditation— The Lord's Prayer

3

Exploring the Spiritual Nature
of Political Systems

Whenever we screw up the courage to face the pain we've been avoiding, we make room for—of all things—joy. Who knew? This is joy we could never have known without coming face-to-face with our pain. It's like a divine alchemy takes place: put our divinity and our distortions into a mortar and pestle, grind away on them for a while, and *poof*, we can turn things back into the good from whence they came. The truth will eventually come out, and we'll find that the hurdles to discovering it aren't nearly as tall as we feared they would be.

So what, pray tell, does this have to do with political systems? We're about to discover, by reviewing the most popular political systems on the planet—monarchy and feudalism, socialism and communism, and capitalistic democracy—that each has a divine origin plus a handful of distortions. But with a little elbow grease, the best in each can be found and enjoyed. We'll also see how each of them—in their divine *and* distorted ways—lives in each one of us.

MONARCHY AND FEUDALISM

The first category, in which we'll combine monarchy and feudalism, is a well known but, by now, obsolete system. The divine origin can be found in certain highly developed people who are fully aware of their responsibilities and are able to enjoy the privileges attached with this. To be sure, we will all discover as we go along that these two things—responsibility and privileges—are bunkmates. In short, if we're willing to shoulder our responsibilities, we get the privileges that match our level of commitment. But we have to earn our right to enjoy the goodies. This is a divine eternal law.

Conversely, if we haven't been willing to assume our rightful responsibilities, well 'no soup for you.' Actually, we're either going to feel too guilty to even want any privileges, or with our rebellious streak, we're going to want to steal them. We will often justify this by claiming the other guy—who actually made the effort to earn their keep—is abusive and unfair. Na-na na-na boo-boo.

Note, when such abuse is aimed at someone in authority, that person who has stepped into assuming the demanding task of leadership doesn't get a free pass to retaliate. For if they have rightfully fulfilled the conditions that would earn them their coveted and envied position—replete with its appropriate privileges—they would have no need to rebel. They will only suffer the envy of others when they have not paid the price for their position of authority.

How about when people give themselves fully to a task such as being head of a government or the leader of a nation? They are acting on their responsibility, in accordance with divine law, to lead and guide those who frankly don't want the job. There are more than a few hardships that come with the territory, along with a matching set of privileges.

Leadership asks for a lot of self-discipline that the self-indulgent aren't really so keen on. Leaders must often give up immediate gratification, which is something their followers would want no part of—even as they are busy resenting the one who leads. Followers also wouldn't be too quick to sign up for the associated risks—risk of exposure, criticism, slander and hostility—that those in the limelight must have the strength to withstand.

Let's face it, it's way easier to be an ordinary citizen than to be the leader of a nation. It's just easier to follow than to lead. Followers can slack—even be a bit lazy—not needing to care that much, try that hard, think that deeply. It simply doesn't take a whole lot of courage to follow.

Leaders, on the other hand, create a following through their devotion to their task and by giving their best; they have the opportunity to use their power for the good of all. True leaders don't shun the many inconveniences connected with their task. This, in a nutshell, describes the divinity that is contained in regimes of monarchy and feudalism.

It's not hard to see how this could be distorted by selfish people who are ruthless and irresponsible; who abuse their position and use it for their own personal power or material gain; who obstruct justice and unfoldment of the law, and block beauty and fairness. But a true monarch who stands solidly at the helm of a ship is always divinely inspired. They must actively seek that inspiration and put it above all else, or abuse will prevail.

Back in the day, when people were generally not well-developed enough to take on the responsibility for governing themselves, these monarchy systems appeared on Earth. People needed to be guided, and so certain highly developed beings were incarnated to fulfill the task of leading them. Sooner or later, though, the temptations became too much for them. Then along came other leaders who took over rulership using force or manipulation, abusing their position and using their power to their advantage.

How does this political system show up in the human psyche? It's not really so hard to detect. First, we each have an innate inner talent to lead in some way, to serve a cause by assuming some type of responsibility. No matter how buried, such talents can be lured out of their dormant state, bringing a person onto their right path.

If we choose not to cultivate our talents, we will then become followers who have fewer rights and privileges. As we wish. But c'mon, if we don't wish to take on the higher calling of leading, standing exposed and risking everything that goes along with this, we don't have a right to complain when others step up.

We can apply this equally to overt outer leadership as much as to very subtle expressions. We might be a school teacher, an office supervisor, or in any other framework a leader, a "monarch"—or simply be a follower. Both roles have their value and are distinctly different. We need to know which one we are choosing.

And we also need to know this: if we are a follower who resists our talent to become a leader in our own right, and we go on to rebel against leadership because we are too lazy, fearful, selfish or self-indulgent, we are as dishonest as the ruler who abuses their power. We commit a grave injustice when we do this.

The term "rulership" refers not only to political expression. Wherever our talents lie, we hold the possibility for higher rulership, in the best sense of this word. And the first place we should be applying it is toward ourselves. This means we need to develop a certain amount of discipline, firmness and strength to not succumb to every whim of our Lower Self.

Temptations to indulge surround us. It is the weak ruler who can't be bothered with healthy discipline, and who does as much damage to themselves as the one who is harsh, close-hearted and overly severe—the one who won't relax their domination. In either case, we can't find the right balance between discipline and relaxation, intuitively knowing when one is right or the other more appropriate.

We won't be able to dish out discipline in a fair and balanced way if we haven't learned to have a little discipline with ourselves. We see this hurtful imbalance in many rulers: self-indulgent with themselves but strict and ruthless with their subjects. A sound spiritual path then must always emphasize—perhaps evenly seemingly over-emphasize—the importance of self-discipline.

We cannot purify and transform distorted aspects of our Lower Self unless we have acquired some self-discipline; we must be vigilant in using it against the ever-lurking resistance to changing and overcoming our own negativity. Only after having mastered our resistance to a considerable degree will our leadership of others evolve organically, perhaps in the form of becoming a spiritual helper, a teacher or someone responsible for leading a community.

So in each soul, both the monarch and the serf exist. One leads and the other follows without taking responsibility. One is rich, the other poor. One has rights, the other has given them up. Which part of ourselves are we feeding? Do we abuse this double principle inside ourselves? The two halves make up one whole, so if we abuse one half, we must also, perforce, abuse the other.

How do we react to that part that wants to cheat, to get results without earning them, to have a free ride without giving anything in return? Or do we take discipline well within ourselves, earning our authority in our immediate environment by the way we lead our lives? Then the "monarch principle" is acting in a harmonious, meaningful way that behaves appropriately toward the "responsible citizen principle" in us. If this is the case, a healthy attitude can manifest in our outer environment and it will stand on solid ground.

Then monarchy and feudalism will arise in their divine sense, not in an abused sense. It must grow like this, from the inside out. We start by cleaning up our own side of the street. Later, once we've established a reasonable amount of self-rulership, we will notice a small sphere of leadership arising naturally, almost as if by itself. It's like a tree: the deeper the roots grow, the further out it is able to extend itself.

As our stature as a leader grows, due to our ongoing development, the sphere of our influence widens and we encompass more "followers" with our positive power. So an organic monarchy that operates harmoniously is a beautiful divine expression in our personal lives that can, in some cases, branch out into public life, if that is so ordained. This explains the way in which the model for the feudal and monarchical political systems fits into the scheme of all things.

SOCIALISM AND COMMUNISM

Once again we will cover two bases at once under the category socialism and communism, which in their divinity are also a part of the grand scheme of things. This probably comes as no surprise when we think of the ideas of equality, fairness and justice for all.

But wait, are people really all the same? Here comes the contradiction: all entities are not equally developed. Some are stronger, some are braver, some are more deserving of the privileged position of leading a country— or a society, or a group of neighbors, or a business, or whatever. So in this sense, people are of course not equal. But then, is this really a contradiction? Absolutely not. How so?

Don't forget, we live here in the land of duality where things often appear as opposites, or contradictions, that really are not. So let's start with this: it is true that people are created equal. Then let's add this: people are not equal in the way they express themselves, in their level of development, or in the direction of their will—in the daily and hourly choices they make regarding their lives. People aren't equal in their thinking, their feeling, their decision-making or their actions.

It's like this: an adult and a child are equal as far as their inherent value as people is concerned. But they're certainly not equal in the way they express themselves in life. So there's no contradiction in saying both are equal, and both are not equal.

In clear reaction to the abuses of the monarchy and feudalism systems, a form of government emerged in which everyone was equalized. The intention was to overcome the abusive inequality characteristic of monarchy and feudalism. In came another facet of divine truth, which was needed to rectify the previous distortions.

But with this second system, abuse once again set in, which is bound to happen whenever one truth is seen as a contradiction to another truth. When the dualistic mind can't find its way to the unitive plane—where not only do contradictions co-exist but both halves are vitally needed to form one complete whole—it sides with one truth and excludes another. This is how we destroy inner unity.

Through our distorted perceptions, we set ourselves on a tightrope where any infringement from "the other side" works to diminish the new truth. Hence, equality becomes abused. A uniformity sets in that no longer honors the vitality of human unfoldment, the diversity of our expressions, or the divergence of our development. Free expression of choice and development of talent is superseded by fairness, uniformity and conformity. One size must fit all.

How does this form of government show up inside our souls? For starters, on the deepest rock-bottom level of our being, we know we're all equals, no matter how distorted or negative someone might be on the surface. If we can resonate with this, our loving nature and common sense will make it possible to pick up on the differences where, on the outer level, there is obviously not so much equality.

Those of us living responsibly and fulfilling our task in the universe, who live our lives according to spiritual laws, are not equal in expression to people who selfishly abuse the laws without concern for how they affect others. It's just not right to say that those who deny divine reality are on par with those who are working to uphold divine truth.

We can only truthfully know this inequality when we also know that deep down, underneath it all, we're all divinely equal. That is essentially the inner expression, in its purity, of the political systems of socialism or communism.

CAPITALISTIC DEMOCRACY

The current popular form of government in countries like the United States is capitalistic democracy. In its original divine nature, it is about to-tal freedom of expression and abundance as it accrues from personal investment. At the same time, the divine form of this system also makes room for caring for those who, for some reason, can't be—or aren't yet willing to be—fully responsible for themselves.

There is no sentimental claim that such people should reap all the same benefits as those who invest their whole being into their lives. But it also doesn't exploit such people to justify the power drive of a ruler. This form of government then is closer to the fusion of duality—to being about uni-ty—and is a more mature form of government than the previous categories (which in practical application, also have sub-categories).

So how do we manage to abuse and distort capitalistic democracy? One aspect is the abuse of power by a stronger few. These are the more willful individuals who impose disadvantages on those who can't or won't stand up for themselves. In truth, disadvantage will be the natural result for people who refuse to fend for themselves; they become parasites at the ex-pense of others. But through the distortions in this system, those who exploit others becomes parasites themselves, using the very ones who want to leach off of others.

Instead of working to help these people wake up and adopt more fair and appropriate ways of being, they play right into their hands. They end up validating the excuses of those who are lazy and cheating, who say it is an unfair world they live in and that they are victimized by the greedy. *Because they are.*

So this system can be abused from both sides. Those clamoring for so-cialism can become more parasitic and blame the power structure for

keeping them down. On the other extreme, those who are strong and diligent, who risk and invest, can justify their greed and drive for power by
blaming the parasitic nature of those who are lazy. But abuse is abuse, regardless of how it dresses for the party.

Because this system offers more possibility for a healthy fusion of two
apparent opposites, it also contains more possibility for abuse; the other
categories offered less freedom, but concomitantly, less possibility for
abuse. That's the paradoxical way of spiritual things: the more developed
and free we become, the greater is the danger for distortion and abuse. As
such, in this system, we find the potential for a "negative fusion" when
both sides are in distortion.

Freedom is funny that way, always containing more and more possibility
for abuse. This is as true inside our souls as in our societies. When abuse
reaches a peak, the painful confusion of duality roars to life and the pendulum—*schwoop*—must go swinging in the opposite direction. Inside ourselves,
we'll go from being a doormat to becoming a raging rebel. Political systems
will swing from authoritarianism in some form to an overly permissive system that lets the parasite make a sentimentality out of their "cause."

Back and forth we go, down through the centuries, until the margin of
the swing narrows and the pendulum approaches the point of fusion. Capitalistic democracy is one such expression. But if this system is heartlessly
governed only by the mind, the possibility for error and yes, abuse, will live
on. What needs to happen is that a channel must open up to perceive divine will and establish divine law.

How can we apply these principles to our inner world? The real question is: when we're given enough leash to responsibly run our own lives, do
we choke ourselves? It's so easy to abuse freedom unless we confront our
hidden motives at all times. It takes more than an ounce of maturity to
abstain from the temptation to abuse freedom when we have it. It takes a
heap of self-discipline.

If we want to stand on our own two feet and avoid becoming a burden
on our fellow-citizens, we'll need maturity as well as strength and fair-
mindedness. It can be tempting to ride on other's coattails, both in our

personal lives and in public life. But every time we give in to this temptation, we draw a tight fence around our emotional freedom, crippling ourselves into no longer feeling free.

We can always find something to blame for our self-restriction, but eventually that dog won't hunt. But we'll keep frantically struggling, unable to understand why we feel so held back, so tied down, so constricted within. We will have unleashed an inner tyrant by constantly abusing our freedom to create, to choose, and to direct our own ship. Yet we won't understand that we're the ones who did this.

WORKING TOGETHER AS ONE

With our knowledge of these three basic systems, knowing their divine meaning and their typical abuses—inside ourselves and out—let's look at how these law apply to everything from seemingly insignificant life stuff to world-scale governments.

First off, politics today has to be led by people who actively cultivate divine inspiration. Now, if we ourselves don't possess such a channel, we're going to have a hard time discerning this in someone else. Perhaps we have a stake in not knowing or maybe we're just being naïve or ignorant, but more and more, people need to collectively come to the realization that this is a thing, and to choose their leaders accordingly. Without personal contact it may be hard to judge any specific leader, but we can call on our own personal inspiration to guide us to intuitively have a sense of this and make good choices.

Certainly, such an assessment is easier to make today than ever before, given our current communication systems. Without a doubt, our technical advancements are yet another facet that reflects the maturing present-day nature of humankind. Beyond this, it is easier today to choose inspired leaders because of the spreading of Christ consciousness throughout the world. It takes a lot of courage for a leader to claim a channel of communication with this power, and also to own up to how hard it is to put self-interest aside. And let's be clear, nothing hoses up a connection with the energy of Christ consciousness more quickly than a self-serving agenda.

With selflessness at the top of the docket, world politics could blend together each one of these political systems, not in contradiction to each other but as one united whole. Indeed, a single government could be created that would combine the divine natures of monarchy and feudalism, socialism and communism, and democratic capitalism. Yes indeedy, it could be done.

For they all contain truth and are in no way contradictory to each other. Their fundamental principles are all living inside each of us right now. As we walk our individual spiritual paths, they each must come into harmony within, blending inside the human personality as seamlessly as they could blend between nations. Such expression could lead to the fullest experiences of creativity, joy and fulfillment ever on this planet.

Taking another tack on this, if we—in our inner government as well as in our world governments—choose not to wisely contain the positive aspects of each of these systems, we'll wipe ourselves out. Any government that can't maintain the balance required for living harmoniously must, sooner or later, be destroyed. And is this not the case, over and over, with each one of us?

For example, it is the struggling person who also strains to be independent, to exaggerate their individuality at the expense of others, to resist conforming. They won't ask for help. Meanwhile, across town, the lazy, demanding person wants to be coddled and given to without the slightest effort on their part. They resent whatever life expects of them, doing only what they can't avoid, but against their will. This is the unruly child that needs a parent's discipline. Neither is in balance.

What's more, tucked away in a corner of our soul is an area that proudly wants to use power to have everything; this part of ourselves doesn't care about anyone else. There is no one who doesn't have some particle of this inside them. If this remains hidden, it will have more power to affect our lives by creating unwanted outcomes. If nothing else, it will create a separating wall of fear and loneliness. We need to face this wall and deal with it, breaking it down and eliminating it. Because it's walls like this that clog up our divine channel. Once this wall is gone, the channel will re-connect automatically.

Just as human beings have been evolving through various stages of development, cleaning up aspects of negativity within, so it is with world politics. Humanity has been fluctuating from one type of political system to another, and we're starting to see that no single system is all good, and none are all bad.

Along the way, we've stubbed our toes on one of the greatest pitfalls of being a human: getting sucked up in the dualistic error that says 'this is right and that is wrong.' Politicians are prime candidates for embracing one form of government as good, and another form as bad. We need to move into a new era in politics where we are not partisan. Further, the new politician's task will be to represent all forms of government known in the world today, *in their divine expression.* For this to happen, politicians will need to open up their connection with the divine and see the unity that exists within apparent contradictions.

As citizens, we need to notice when we are rebelling against one aspect of a political system in favor of another. When that happens, we don't get to pass Go; we're already in distortion. (And the $200? Fuhgeddaboudit.) So we can use our rebellion as a reminder to look within, searching for what's out of whack. Is it the lazy part that resents authority and doesn't want to have to pay a price *for anything?* Could it be the envious part that refuses to step up to the plate and earn what it envies? Maybe it's the powerful part that secretly wishes to abuse power?

Similar to the way we approach finding inner unity—seeking "both/and" instead of tripping over "either/or"—we can search for harmony in our governing bodies by totally surrendering to the will of the highest. Where is God in this or that specific issue? How open are we to finding the truth? What holds us back from surrendering to divine will? And how can we ask for such willingness to surrender in our leaders when we refuse it in ourselves? The work of clearing always begins in our own backyard.

Unity holds greater truths than we can dream of when we're caught in a web of duality. But until we cultivate a vision to see things on the unitive plane of reality, these truths can't reveal themselves to us. We need to shift to this broader perspective if we want to build a beautiful new world together.

#242 The Spiritual Meaning of Political Systems

4

Debunking the Curious
Superstition of Pessimism

Whether we think of ourselves as spiritual or religious, atheistic or None of the Above, we all have one thing in common: we humans are a superstitious lot. There is one insidious form of superstition—pessimism—that is the hidden culprit behind many of our disappointments in life.

It all starts with an inner attitude that goes something like this: "If I believe that something good may happen, I will be disappointed because I will chase it away with my believing in it. Maybe it's a safer bet to believe that nothing good will happen to me—that I can't change and have a better life." This is the game we play with ourselves. It has a deliberate but destructive playfulness to it that is based purely on superstition.

Now, for most of us, we're beyond believing in primitive superstitions. But nonetheless such subtler varieties do exist in nearly all of us. This one is buried in the voice that says, "I'd better not believe in the good because it might not happen." Listen for it, because it's in there; we need to hear these words.

At some point, this playful game starts to go sideways and then the fun gets lost in its tragically painful effects. It turns out that denying the positive and believing in the worst—as though to appease the gods—is downright destructive. Because there is power in our thoughts, and there's

33

no playing with that power without getting hurt.

There's no limit to the many things we might be applying this to in life. Perhaps it's regarding the healing of an illness. Or when we're alone and feeling unloved, we might playfully—safely, we think—tell others and ourselves that we'll always be alone. Maybe we're lacking funds or the satisfaction of a fulfilling profession, so we comfort ourselves by saying "I'm going to believe it has to be this way, so then maybe it can come to me out of the blue." It's like we're hoping for some perfect parent to magically materialize and whisk away our doubts saying "Oh no, dear child, it's not that bad. See, everything is going to be wonderful." Exclamation point.

Unbeknownst to us, we are directing our soul with a belief that will create circumstances that prove it. But then we "forget" that we were playing a game, all in a spirit of superstition—or maybe like a spirit of emotional manipulation. After a while, we get so far down the rabbit hole, we begin to believe that the negative manifestation is reality. So what started as a fun little superstitious safety valve has turned into a belief on another level of our awareness. This is what now creates reality and keeps us stuck in a lousy place. Curiouser and curiouser.

All such mental trickery is quite dangerous. We are abusing the power of the word, the power of our own thinking, and the power of teaching ourselves untruths. Whenever we come across this kind of self-deception, we have to stop, drop and roll before we get burned any further. We can objectively observe where and how we have done this to ourselves, and connect with our intention behind these maneuvers.

Next, hold up a stop-sign-to-self and say, "I want to stop fooling myself this way. Life can't be cheated or tricked. I choose honesty from here on out. I must mean what I say to myself on the deepest levels of myself. It has to jive with the truth of life." We need to counter our habit of tricking ourselves, wherever it exists in us, by finding new pathways for our minds to follow.

This next step is the real nut. On the surface it may sound simple but it may also require us to marshal a fair bit of courage—the courage to believe in the good. This is what is called an "abyss of illusion." Without any assurances that things are all going to turn out fine, we're going to have to venture into unknown territory where we believe in the positive. We'll need to assert that we have faith that the universe is totally benign—good and loving and safe. We'll need to express the truth that there are infinite possibilities for what can happen. Gleeps.

We can pick our path: the road of Eeyore-style gloom, denial and defeatism, or the road of faith in the innate nature of life to unfold with beautiful possibilities. The anchor holding us back from manifesting awesome possibilities lies in our own soul. There's nothing we can't realize if we truly give ourselves to it; there's nothing we can't experience. We have the power to remove the anchor. Then involuntary processes will carry us to new shores of fulfillment riding on the wave of limitless creative possibilities. The only question is: do we have the courage to bridge the gap by way of a faith that must wait for our inner spirit to reset the sails?

The nice thing about our old superstitions is that we just speak negative beliefs and they come true. No waiting. For certain, the questionable results we're so keen on will happen immediately. It's tempting to lean on that instead of investing in a very uncertain waiting period.

For the journey to having faith in a positive unfoldment takes a bit of time to ripen. This is so because our mental processes need to do a one-eighty, readjusting themselves so they can take root in the new land of abundance. We need the patience of a gardener who understands that a gestation period is required. With experience, the gardener learns that after sowing seeds, one must wait for the plants to sprout. It would be hard to trust this process until we've seen it in action.

So it is with each of us. That first step of faith can be a doozy.

There is a pitfall to watch out for: it's easy to confuse this courage of which we speak—a vigorous faith in good outcomes—with wishful thinking. But they're not the same. Many of us indulge in wishful thinking at the drop of a hat. Then, to be "realisitic"—because we know how darned disappointing the results of wishful thinking are apt to be—we scurry back to a known quantity: our pessimistic superstitions.

How do we distinguish between the two? Fortunately, there is a one clear and simple factor that will allows us to distinctly distinguish between them. With wishful thinking, we spin fantastic dreams of fulfillment without having any price to pay: no change is expected in our approach or attitude, thinking or feeling, acting or being. In our daydreams, happiness comes our way magically and gratuitously, and we don't have to make any investment in the creative process for it to happen. We think we can game the system, not having to contribute to the evolutionary plan through a commitment to purifying our own souls.

No, in wishful thinking, we get to be totally passive, hoping against hope that something wonderful will come our way and we won't have to lift a finger to remove the very block that is preventing the desirable thing we dream about. Easy peasy lemon squeezy. But when all is said and done, the less we invest in turning a desirable event or state into a reality, the less we ourselves even believe it will happen.

It's like a teeter-totter: the more we justify our superstition of pessimism, the less desirable our life becomes. More and more, we will want to escape from our dreary creations by spinning daydreams that sub for reality. Believe it or not, this chews up a lot of creative energy that could be better invested in doing something real and helpful. Daydreams, then, are nothing more than the flipside of the superstition of pessimism.

On the same day—heck, maybe even in the same hour—we will waffle between these two, indulging in daydreams and then plunging minutes later into superstitious beliefs that only bad will come our way. But what if we took all that mischanneled energy and creativity and sunk it into a commitment to life and ourselves? We could actually then accomplish the very thing we are daydreaming about, and start giving our best to both— which, in the end, are one and the same.

Instead, what happens is that we fail to come around on our daydreams—big surprise there—and our disappoint fortifies our pessimism. The game comes to life, sealing the deal on our wrong, negative beliefs. Now something called a vicious circle takes up residence and gains momentum, making it harder and harder to extricate ourselves from the game. The pendulum swings between thoughts of bad juju and fantastical daydreams, using one to escape the outcome of the other. Neither delivers an iota of abundance, joy, beauty, love or excitement.

What aspect of ourselves spins these wishful daydreams? They come from an undeveloped ego, not from desires of the Higher Self, or inner spirit. The weak ego is looking for a magic pill that will save it from its own underdevelopment. So, for example, instead of seeing ourselves in a productive career, contributing in a meaningful way and gaining success as a fruit of our labor, we dream of being a great person who impresses others—like our family or the people who have slighted us. Feel the difference?

Let's look for the grain of truth under this kind of ego gratification: our desire to experience our true value. We all have dignity, but when we confuse it with the petty pride of our limited ego, it gets displaced. We're aiming for the rich fulfillment that comes from things like recognition and respect, along with friendship, communication and abundance. But in daydreams, we acquire these things in a fairy tale manner. This is so unconvincing—even to us—that of course we can't then believe they're true.

As we do the work of uncovering our Lower Self and unwinding the negativity it holds, the temptation to indulge in daydreams will naturally diminish. Once we start dealing more in reality, life will become more real. Wherever the habit persists, we need to look deeper. Where do we hope for a knight in shining armor to rush in and take our cares away? How are we still hoping that a super-authority will do our work for us and ta-da, the world will be our oyster without our having to earn it.

If we allow ourselves to bring these thoughts out of the ether and into our conscious mind—perhaps writing them down to see them in black and white—we will see their absurdity. This alone will help us give them up. Once we become willing to squander ourselves into life, giving of our inner riches as generously as we want life to give to us, we'll realize that abundance can be ours.

The road to waking up is not a direct shot. It's two steps forward and one step back; it curves from side to side. We don't find happiness and pleasure once and sustain it for all time. We find it, lose it, and then have to find it again. When we lose it, we often shrink back. This isn't just an old habit. It's the result of our commitment to the make-believe safety net of this superstition of pessimism, countered with an escape into wishful daydreaming.

Becoming aware of this is immeasurably important. We have to see this mechanism for the trick that it is. Then we have to give up this trick. We need to find the courage to believe in our own riches, and have faith in the best life can be.

Every tiny step of goodwill we take, every time we face the worst in us and restore our original beauty, we add to the great reservoir of creative forces. This is how we each do our part in helping the Christ force live and breathe. As we aid our own happiness, we contribute something powerful and valuable to the universe. Great good comes from our willingness to face ourselves and be in truth.

#236 The Superstition of Pessimism

5

Preparing for Reincarnation:
Every Life Counts

From the Spirit World's perspective, birth is no small thing. Even talking about it is a major challenge, trying to squeeze explanations of an exceptionally complicated procedure into language 3D-humans can understand. This overview, then, is intended only as a rough sketch of the process. So go easy here. We'll start by talking about the spiritual and psychological conditions of the birth process, which relate to karmic law. Then we'll see how the technical aspect of birthing is directly connected with this.

Consider this: our next life has already been teed up, at least to some extent. And we're the ones who do this. Nothing's set in stone though, since up until our very last breath things could still change. There's a really good chance, in fact, for that to happen—way more so while still in our bodies than once we get back to the other side.

Once we pass through those pearly gates, we'll be able to make a few minor adjustments to our Next Life Plan, but at that point, only small ones. What's the hold up? It's just that life there, in the Spirit World, is easier than it is on Earth. And that's why development happens more slowly there. So it's definitely more difficult to wait until we're there to try to effect a change.

Up until a certain point in our development, we aren't actually allowed to make too many decisions on our own. But then we reach a certain stage, as we make our way through the cycles of birth-death-and-rebirth, when we have the right—nay, we have the *duty*—to help decide what the circumstances of our next life should be. And depending on our personality, these decisions may or may not be good ones.

It's hard not to notice that sometimes we humans are just really darned lazy. We lack ambition and are satisfied with having a certain amount of comfort. So then we don't work too hard to reach higher levels of consciousness or happiness. If that's us—*slackers*—we're going to opt for an easier life than would be good for us. We don't yet have a very good grip on what the whole purpose of coming to Earth is about.

And then there's that other type—the classic Type A personality—who is overambitious and overactive. Such overachievers will tend to bite off more than they can chew. This too hinders progress and can cause a temporary setback. In this case, the individual is not able to accurately assess their own limitations. Long story short, both the overly optimistic and the overly pessimistic type are at risk for using poor judgment.

Any extremes in our character will result in a lack of harmony, and that's what influences proper judgment. So we need to find the middle of the road before we become at all reliable in our decision-making abilities. Until we mature to such a level of development, higher authorities will make decisions on our behalf.

To be sure, even then we are consulted about what we imagine would be in our best interest for our next incarnation. This is actually a test, and afterward it is explained to us why our less-than-stellar ideas wouldn't pan out so well—might even be dangerous. Hence, at this stage of the game, the decisions are mostly made by highly developed spirits who are trained in such matters and who can help assure a stronger chance for advancement.

Schooling, then, doesn't stop after Earth-school; it's inherent in the planning process for determining our Next Life. So if we learn nothing while we're here, we'll be schooled by this process alone. It's a gradual process with no definite border between when we're ready to make our decisions and when we're not. As such, it may well happen that some of our ideas are usable, and then they will be adopted; others still may need to be rejected. Slowly we learn, incarnation after incarnation, so that more and more of our ideas can be factored in.

Along the way, while we're still riding the rails between suggestions for lives that would be too rough and others that would be a cakewalk, our advisors will offer us other alternatives. Then, according to our free will, we can either accept or reject the advice. Should we reject their good advice, we'll get a chance to review how things turned out and see the effect of our faulty judgment. What a great learning opportunity—possibly the only way we were going to learn our lesson.

For we might never have been convinced of the error in our thinking if we hadn't been given the chance to make a mistake. At the same time, we're protected from ourselves; if the case is too hopeless or would create too much of a disaster, the following of our wishes will be postponed. There is so much that is carefully considered.

Failing or succeeding at our Life Plan, regardless of whether we planned the incarnation or a higher authority did, determines the speed of our development. We might speed things up or slow things down, but it's never a one-shot deal. Life on Earth involves a long series of lives, with each life nothing but a small link in the chain. And the evaluation of our performance—whether or not we met our duties and fulfilled our task—will depend on many, many circumstances.

We each have a Book of Life and everything gets written down in it. It is a record of everything there is to know about us: our special talents, our inclinations, our personality trends and the characteristics that led us to fall from grace in the first place. All these things are inscribed and continually updated. It also tracks our progress since the Fall, including our Earth activities and whatever we have done in between incarnations.

Every incarnation is meticulously planned by carefully following the information contained in our "general ledger." And before each incarnation, we get to take a look at the whole thing. Even if we can't yet make our own decisions, we are allowed to see the purpose of what we're supposed to accomplish in the upcoming trip to Earth-town.

Karma, or the law of cause and effect, doesn't always work itself out from one life to the next. Often, a cause from one life will only produce an effect three or four lifetimes later. This happens because we are never required to bear too much at one time. Generally speaking though, the further we are in our development, the more quickly will the effect follow the cause. But it doesn't always go that way, so be careful about comparing, judging and generalizing. Our view is very limited, seeing just one life at a time, and at that, what we see is still even more limited. This makes it extremely foolish to think we can be the judge and jury on how justice works regarding God's laws.

So whenever we're inclined to say that our life is too difficult to bear or that someone else has it too easy, we need to back off. We wouldn't think this for a minute if we saw all the missing puzzle pieces. Further, it is with good reason that the curtains are drawn on all this. It must be this way until we have personally gained a state of consciousness where having behind-the-scenes information would be good for us and those around us. So have some humility and don't be hatin'.

In fact, write this in big, bold letters on your mirror: NEVER JUDGE. We simply can't compare our life with anyone else's, or the fates of any two people we know. If it seems like we're being asked to carry a heavier cross, it's because more can be expected of us. We are stronger, which means we're further up the ladder. Or maybe, if we happen to be one of those particularly ambitious people, we have chosen to take on an unnecessarily tough life. We may have even gone against the advice of wiser souls. Think long and hard about this, people.

We said earlier that our next incarnation is already in the queue; plans are being made. The thing that most determines what opportunities we will get to next—and what we need to work on for our overall development—is how much of our current plan we fulfill. If we don't advance much this time around or we do a rather half-assed job of it, we may be looking at a complete do-over. Or possibly a partial.

On the other hand, we sometimes have a motor in our butt and we accomplish more in our lifetime than we set out to do. Or maybe we wrap things up early. Good news if that's case, because then we can get started on what we teed up for next time. This will change the blueprint for our next incarnation of course, but no worries, that was always subject to change. It ain't over till it's over.

Again, don't jump to judgment; an easy, pleasant life may not indicate that the previous one was gangbusters. It could be that merits were earned, possibly three or four lifetimes back. Likewise, a tough life might be the result of actions in our last incarnation. Or not. A zealous person may make the choice to pay off, in one lifetime, a monster demerit, while another pays off just as great a demerit—maybe even a bigger one—but eats the elephant one bite at a time. So one more time, what did we say about comparing and judging?

All this is good food for thought. We can sit with this material in meditation realizing that we have so many chances to do things differently for the betterment of our Life Plan. We can annul bad karma we've accumulated over the eons, and we can do this so much quicker if we grasp the point of what life is all about.

Regardless how we play our cards, one day we will die an earthly death. After we wrap up things up here, an accounting will be made, with every little minutia thoroughly and justly checked so there can be no argument about it. In the Spirit World, everything is out in the open and it can never be that one opinion opposes another.

There, everything has definite form, including our thoughts, feelings, reactions, attitudes and deeds. These are as visible and substantial there as a table or a chair here. Actually, they are more so. So they can't be argued about. It would be like two normal people arguing about whether a table is a circle or a square; this is not a matter of opinion.

So the forms of our incarnation cannot be argued about, which isn't to say that arguments aren't allowed. But when the truth is sitting there right before our eyes, well, we simply can't keep denying it and deceiving ourselves the way we do when we are hidden behind matter.

So a full accounting is made and carefully considered. A side-by-side is done with the original plan for this incarnation, along with a look at our overall plan. If we did good, the negative trends and faults we overcame will get checked off the list. It will be noted that we fulfilled our task. Next up: nail down plans for the next outing.

There's a pretty long gap, by human standards, between incarnations, typically in the 300-year range. Many spirits need to take a breather and rest, especially if they've suffered a lot—physically, mentally or otherwise. The time of accounting may occur either before or after the rest period. Then we're back to school, enrolling in classes according to our personal needs. We then each end up hanging out in a sphere that matches our level of purification. Actually, the sequence of these events may vary, as there is no rule governing how these phases proceed.

While we're in the Spirit World, we often do our purification work in connection with souls who are incarnated as humans, which may seem odd to hear. For example, say we were supposed to straighten out a particular relationship during our last visit to Earth. But we didn't get it done; we never learned to love and accept this person. It may now still be possible to finish this task, which could happen through a variety of different means.

It also happens that in our time between incarnations, we may do service work, pitching in to help the Plan of Salvation if we're far enough along ourselves to be helpful. Or we may work on purifying ourselves further during our time in one of the spheres that exists on many different levels in the beyond.

All of these phases—fulfilling tasks, purifying ourselves, summarizing the last incarnation, planning for the next—may overlap or be sharply divided. Note, all this is only true for those spirits who have volunteered to be part of the Divine Order. There are other souls who are still trying to make it on their own. They too have an accounting and planning department, but it's on a lower level, so to speak. Free will being what it is, all the same principles apply but not in the same way.

An entity's decision to become part of the Divine Order—or not—has a big impact on both their time in the Spirit World and on what their incarnations will look like. As our spiritual consciousness is lifted, we'll be able to discern which group we are in. In all cases, justice is always preserved.

If we still find ourselves in the cycle of incarnations, as nearly all humans do, the time will come to be reborn. Once again we meet with the authorities who have helped arrange all our previous visits and filed our post-Earth-journey paperwork. The bookmarked plans for the next life are reviewed and changed as appropriate.

The preparation of the final plan takes considerable time and all choices must be made in the most practical way. The right parents have to be chosen, along with the nationality, religion and life circumstances; certain "fated" life phases must be considered and figured in. For instance, if there are certain disharmonies in the soul, the parents are selected who will create the best environment for bringing this out. This means that particular imperfections will be needed in the child's environment. For if everything were perfect, the shortcomings wouldn't get a chance to surface and be healed. Then why bother coming to Earth at all? At the same time, the parents may have a karmic link to this spirit, so it may be time to pay off a karmic debt.

Upsides and downsides in the upcoming life are weighed against the overall plan. How much should the entity take on? Which character trends need the most attention? Those who are highly developed and able to take on a task for the Plan of Salvation will factor this in with their own personal work. Some talents will be brought front and center, while others are slated to remain hidden this time around. The entity then gets to add their two cents, and if they aren't yet capable of adding even that much, they at least get to share what they'd choose if they could. All this is painstakingly studied, processed, explained and reviewed.

Finally, a plan comes together. Special spirits are then sent out to various places, including Earth, to prepare the way using guidance and inspiration. Occasionally they must report back with bad news: things are not as expected and won't be suitable for the purpose of this incarnation. Then other karmic ties are brought forward into this life that would otherwise have waited for a future opportunity.

OK, now the plan is really coming together. Conditions are checked. Preparations are made. The entity is then led into a different sphere. Think of this like a really great hospital where spiritual physicians are working. In fact, many of our physicians here on Earth have come from this place—which exists on many levels—where they have spent time learning.

There are also many spirits working in this place who are out of the cycles of incarnation, as well as many who never participated in the Fall. They have the responsible task of mentoring other spirits. There are many different departments in this hospital-like sphere. One, for example, handles spirits who have died in accidents or whose life ended abruptly in a violent death. In such cases, their fluid bodies may have been injured and they require special care to nurse them back to health, if you will. Then they are ready to resume their activities in the Spirit World.

In another large area, the entity to be incarnated is brought into contact with their guardian spirit or spirits. This could be a familiar old face or someone new. This guardian delivers the action plan to the spirit in charge of this sphere, who thoroughly reviews everything again. Then assistants are called in to work on the incarnating entity. The plans are intricately poured over and preparations are made.

Let's pause here. Does this all sound impossible? Too human? Too concrete to be believed? Have you heard the one about truth being stranger than fiction? Well, this is the way it is. Of course, it is quite different from how things are done on Earth; it's not exactly the way our minds might imagine. The words used to describe all this create close facsimiles but not exact replicas.

But all this exists: hospital spheres and spirit physicians, high-level authorities and able assistants, general ledgers and specific Life Plans. For nothing exists here on planet Earth that is not a poor copy of what already exists in the Spirit World, even if in a somewhat modified way.

So back to the plans. When everything is in order, the entity waits for conception to occur. For this aspect, astrological factors must be considered. Also, nothing—absolutely nothing—happens if it's not God's will—

including the conception. Perhaps the timing isn't quite right yet for the incoming entity. Then it will be prevented by spiritual means but may happen with these parents the next month.

The complexity of how the specific so-called genes of the parents are called into play is beyond difficult to explain. Suffice it to say, they are studied in depth and must align with the entity coming in; they are governed partly automatically as an effect of causes set in motion, and partly according to certain magnetic fields, rays and fluids which are administered by spirit helpers.

Once conception happens, the incoming entity goes blank. In such a state of unconsciousness, a great part of this soul's knowledge goes dormant and will only come back after this life on Earth is complete. Other parts may come back during Earth-life, but only when the entity leaves the body, as happens during sleep. During the process of growing up, consciousness will also awaken. This all happens according to how the spirit physicians have prepared certain types of personality-related fluids in the entity.

The genes, as we know, affect the physical shell of the being to be incarnated. The baby's body, then, is growing inside the mother's body in such a way that physical karmic aspects will be fulfilled. Nothing is left to coincidence. Nothing is left to itself. When it says in the Bible that God has counted every single hair on our heads, we can believe it.

There is no detail that doesn't correspond, that doesn't have meaning and a deeper significance than we can ever possibly guess. We have our notions about symbolism backwards. Our bodies are symbols of our spiritual development and psychological trends; they are an out-picturing of what's inside. But be ever so careful about making generalizations. No rules apply.

Back to the genes—they are worked on to assure that the shell, or body, is properly prepared. Some genes are going to have an influence, others will not. Sometimes the mother's genes are in the lead, and sometimes it's the father's. At one time, the parent's genes may not activate at all, but then those of a grandparent or great aunt may suddenly switch on. This is never arbitrary or left to chance. For each and every detail, there is a reason.

At this point, as the baby's body grows within the mother, there is no spirit in it. Everything is proceeding however exactly according to plan. In addition to the preparations for the physical body, other highly trained specialists have concentrated on preparing the psychological and spiritual factors. Through their treatment of other certain fluids, some consciousness will return to the person as they grow, while other types of consciousness are destined to remain hidden.

And so it is that one person grows up feeling a strong connection to God, even though they may have atheistic or materialistic parents. In another case, it's just the opposite. Maybe there will be a strong urge to become a painter or a physicist, despite early influences to the contrary. All this is related to how these fluids have been prepared prior to birth.

Sometimes a fluid is prepared to assure that an urge, trend or leaning will surface at some appointed period. Other fluids might be prepared in such a way that certain conditions must be met first. Does this give a glimpse of how infinitely complicated and exacting this preparation process must be for every incarnating soul?

The faults we plan to work on in our lifetime are like currents of energy. These live wires will be meticulously laid down in the fluid bodies in such a way that it won't take much to bring them out. Again, just the right parents and life situations will have been selected to assure that those next up for transformation won't be overlooked. Some others are supposed to remain hidden, to be worked on in the future or only if the plan for this life gets completed ahead of schedule. Thankfully there are experts who skillfully prepare for every contingency.

We can use this information to explain what might be happening when a friend or loved one suddenly displays new and unusual traits. Perhaps they were a decent person who was conscientious about their shortcomings and seemed to be making good progress on their spiritual path. Then wham, they turn into a jerk. We're shocked and dismayed at this turn of behavior, having thought they were working quite well, spiritually speaking. Maybe they really were making progress and now more deeply buried trends are surfacing for purification. It's not uncommon, in fact, for someone on a spiritual path to seem to go rogue, as it were.

Positive traits and talents are treated similarly to faults—some will surface readily and others only after definite conditions are fulfilled. Clear a hurdle and then a door opens within. It may be we have full-on access from a young age. Or we may need to show we will stay on task before we earn access to our own gifts. It's all there on our chart, although with ridiculously more complexity than can even be hinted at here.

This processing and treatment of our fluid bodies, in preparation for the Big Day, takes about nine Earth-months to complete. Sounds about right. When things get wrapped up early, the baby just hangs out and waits in an unconscious state. As we know, sometimes the little one arrives ahead of schedule, if the conditions for beginning life are more suitable then. Or it could be the parents need to experience a premature birth—or a late arrival—to fulfill some karmic conditions. Always, always, always it goes according to a plan.

Here's one final detail to consider. During the pregnancy, the attitudes of both the mother and the father may result in a change order. If either has an adjustment in their spiritual attitude during this time, the arriving entity may no longer be the best match. Perhaps the parents would now be best suited with a more highly developed spirit as their child. Or maybe they would no longer serve to bring out the issues of the incoming entity, now that they have a more spiritualized outlook on things.

There are plenty of parents to choose from who offer the limitations needed for growth. Far fewer can offer the right environment for an entity who will have more to give to the world. Such a task carries certain responsibilities for these parents; they must be worthy of rearing a child who has a greater task to fulfill. This worthiness is often determined by the spiritual outlook such a person has about life.

So if changes occur in the parents—for better or for worse—last-minute changes can be made. As we might expect, plans have been made to accommodate every eventuality. Remember, in the Spirit World, our Book of Life is available for perusing, so much more is known about what's in the realm of possibility than we can foretell with our human senses.

When a switch to a different child must be made, the first intended child will proceed without delay or difficulty to another pregnant woman. Therefore, expecting mothers are encouraged to spend time becoming quiet within, turning to God and focusing on spiritualizing their whole being during this important time. Then when the exciting moment of birth finally arrives, many spirits are called on to assist in placing the carefully prepared fluid bodies into the body of the baby.

It is with such intricate and intimate care that we are tended to when preparing for our next incarnation to begin. Welcome back.

#34 Preparation for Reincarnation

6

Unwinding Humanity's Relationship with Time

We may talk a good game about living in the present, but then turn around and face periods of depression, anxiety, uncertainty and disharmony. Hey, who wants to be present with that? So we keep turning away only to find ourselves lost in a maze of unhappy emotions. OK, uncle. Now how do we find our way out?

It's like this. Imagine we live in a great big house that has one room we don't use, so it becomes a room for storage. We push a few things into it helter-skelter and if we had to tidy it up at that point, it wouldn't take too long.

Imagine over time we let things pile up until that room's filled to the brim. We're lazy and don't want to hassle with sorting things and putting them away as we go. Now we've got a tougher job on our hands. It's just like this with the time we have at our disposal.

If we have a problem area and at the first sign of feeling troubled we heed it saying, "Now what am I really feeling? Why am I just a little disturbed?"—rather than packing it away into the storeroom of our unawareness—we will be able to sort out what it's about in jig time.

But if instead we let it ride, pushing it out of our mind, it will fester underground. Now it starts to create negative patterns and vicious circles that seem to trap us in wicked chain reactions that eat our lunch. These snowball into whole interwoven knots that become very hard to disentangle.

The snowball grows, we drop lower down the scale of Big Bad Moods, and it becomes increasingly more difficult to restore things to order.

Now it will take much greater effort to undo the knots of wrong thinking, negative effects and painful interactions that have sent our energy currents into destructive neighborhoods they shouldn't have gone into. Jeez, what a huge waste of time. This will now take so much work to sort out, we turn the other way and let things pile up some more. Until *Pop!* goes the weasel.

This, folks, is why we need to learn to make better use of our time, especially when we feel any discomfort or disharmony. And this is also why it is nuts for us to believe bad times are such a hardship. In truth, the only way to safeguard ourselves against further future misery is by letting ourselves get shaken up by our struggles. We can use them to bring out whatever is hidden. In fact, we can only uncover what needs healing by facing all that touches us.

If we heed the little signs, we can do a little shoveling as we go and the messes won't build up. The problem is we wait—often through one incarnation after another—before we look at ourselves in truth. We'd rather say we're haunted by bad luck or are the sorry victim of someone else's malice than look at what we don't wish to see in ourselves.

Human beings living on Earth are bound by time, which is a creation of the mind. Without our minds, time wouldn't exist. Beyond this, we live in a dimension where time is a separate element from space and movement. But later in our development, as we reach higher degrees of awareness, our reality will shift, more and more, to where time, space and movement become integrated into one.

To help make this more clear, consider that in our dimension, time and space are two separate factors. If we are located in a certain *space*, it will take *time* to move to another space. *Movement* is the bridge that combines time and space. In the next dimension, where the fragment of time is what we might call "wider," movement, time and space are one. So if we're in one space, we only need to have a new thought to be in another space. Movement is not required; the thought is the bridge and it is of a shorter span of time and motion.

Given the material nature of life on Earth, we cannot bridge distance with thought, although our spirit—or psyche—experiences this constantly, even if the brain doesn't think of it in these terms. Currently, however, the human body is bound by a separation between time and space that can only be bridged by movement.

When material and technical means are invented to leave this dimension, we will have an inkling of what is going on here. Certainly it is a reflection of our overall readiness to grasp higher truth that we have gained our current level of technical astuteness, bringing us closer to this possibility. But that doesn't mean we will automatically grasp the more profound meaning; that all depends on people's willingness and capacity to understand.

And if, in spite of our growth, we don't learn the deeper meaning, our discoveries will stagnate and turn destructive instead of helping humanity gain broader awareness. The litmus test for whether a scientific discovery—or really any influx of knowledge, perhaps in art or philosophy—will be beneficial depends on whether humanity understands cosmic law better after its unfolding than before. If so, it will lead to greater freedoms, faster growth, and more peace and justice.

If we looked at history from this point of view, we would see that every upheaval on planet Earth has resulted from an ignorance about the real meaning of a new broader knowledge. For historians to identify these links, they themselves will need to be undertaking a self-searching process of personal development. Then dots that were previously obscure will start to line up.

Coming back to the topic of time, it's not quite right to say the next higher dimension is timelessness. There is a spectrum of time-realities we will experience on our way to timelessness. Our current position on this spectrum, as humans, makes it hard to fully grasp this; the best we can do is sense this truth occasionally.

Time is a fragment, cut from a wider, freer cloth of experience. As such, time is very limiting. At the same time, it has the benefit of motivating us to grow and fulfill ourselves, moving us toward the maximum happiness and freedom we can hope for in this dimension. If we work it right, we will reach our potential, and in that case, the limitation of time won't be a hardship. On the other hand, a person who has a potential to grow but doesn't use it, will be a more troubled soul than someone who exerts less effort but is working closer to their given potential. This is why we should try to stay off the judging committee.

If we have consciously embarked on a spiritual path of personal development, it is possible that we will still miss the boat from time to time. We'll gut our way through a rough patch without taking the time to explore what it's about, just waiting for it to pass on its own. When we overlook our bad moods, we invite depression, anxiety, uncertainty and disharmony to come calling again and again. These are the occasions when we are not using time well and it must become a source of conflict and a burden.

But if we search for the root of our problems, we will unfurl the deeper understanding that leads to liberation. Then our trust in life gets established in firm soil, and our exhilaration in ourselves becomes a more permanent state instead of a periodic one-off. We will organically become, more and more, at one with the element of time.

In the last analysis, we can look at any unwelcome emotion as a result of not using our time wisely in getting to the bottom of inner conflicts and confusions. These include boredom and apathy, frustration and tension, anxiety and hostility, impatience and nervousness, listlessness and depression.

Those who are already fairly far along on their path of self-discovery will know of the influx of joy and strength that comes from unraveling any issue all the way to the origin of the negative emotion. Those who haven't yet had this experience should know that this could be yours if you are willing to follow the threads of your own inconvenient feelings. We just need to not shirk the effort of looking within, which will lead us to this feeling that we are one with life.

We may be saying, "Remind me, what does any of this have to do with our relationship to time?" Here it is: any negative emotion essentially conflicts with the limited fragment of time we have. Conversely, feelings that are positive, constructive and realistic don't conflict with time because we're using time the way it's supposed to be used. This is good fodder for deep meditation.

Our vague awareness that time is limited creates a special tension in us. Therefore we strain against time like a dog pulls on a leash; it holds us in its grip and we feel strangled by it. In our unconscious minds, we hold a memory of another greater timelessness where we had limitless freedom. But we can only get back there by fully accepting and utilizing the fragments of time we now have.

So we can do it either way: transition into freedom organically with a minimum of conflict, or keep straining against the transition. Said another way, we can face tensions and conflicts head on and find freedom, or we can live with the tension and conflicts created by our avoidance—our improper use of our time—and stay stuck. Our choice.

Why should we believe any of this is true? Fortunately, there is a simple way to test whether any spiritual concept is truthful: does it have any practical application. If we can't take an idea and test-drive it, what good is it really? So let's look at this topic of time as it relates to people on a day-to-day basis.

In our everyday reality, we attempt to reach that freer dimension of time by striving toward tomorrow. Sometimes this is obvious just by looking at our surface thoughts; at other times there is just a vague general climate of leash tugging that is hard to pinpoint.

We strive toward the future for mainly two reasons. First, we're not crazy about the present and we hope the future might offer us something better. Or second, there is some aspect of life we fear and we want to leave it in the past. So we have this fuzzy belief in a happier future coupled with some dissatisfaction or annoyance about the present that causes us to avoid living in the Now.

We've got to learn to fully milk each moment for what it can teach us. This is where the rubber meets the road. If we were to explore each difficulty fully, instead of straining away from them, we would be living each moment to the fullest. Plus, it's only by fully utilizing the fragments of time we are given in this dimension that we can outgrow them. Experiencing everything, then, and not straining away is the way to automatically flow into the next time-dimension.

In this directive to live in the Now, great confusion arises regarding using our time to reflect on the past or to plan for the future. As with everything, there is A) what we do, and B) how we go about it. B is scads more important than A. So we can think about the past in a constructive way to help us understand ourselves and our present problems better, and this will help us resolve them so we are better equipped to live in the Now. Or, if we prefer, we can run in circles and hold onto the past, thinking about it in a destructive way; we can sit around blaming fate or some other shmuck for some unpleasantness in our life; we can just be haters, preoccupied with resenting the past. It's up to us.

Same for the future. We may, on one hand, take responsibility for our future in a flexible way that doesn't fixate on it. Or we can hang out forever in some hazy future tense that never quite becomes the Now. Or when it does, the disillusionment is tremendous; *this isn't how we fantasized it would be.*

No, it's not impossible to experience happiness in the Now, but to do so we need to not run from whatever is unwelcome in the present. This could be fear, doubt, self-dislike, resentments or loneliness—whatever it is, it's all fair game for further exploration. But whenever we're busy running from what's disturbing, we can't be present for whatever might be beautiful in the moment.

For example, let's say we have a tendency to worry. We think, "My goodness, if I face my worry, I won't be able to be present in the Now." So we run from it. Instead we could try saying, "I am worried about thus-and-such, and even though I know it is irrational, this is how I feel. I feel worried in this moment." Then a relaxation can happen because we are being present with the worry. We will still have the worry, but it will feel less disturbing, which will create some space for possibly understanding the worry and proceeding from there.

Our misunderstanding is that we think we shouldn't have the worry. In that moment, we are not in reality; we are not present with what actually is. *This* is the problem—not the worry. We think we must first free ourselves of our problems before we can live in some faraway spiritual land of the Now. It doesn't work that way. And it never will.

We are mistaken when we believe that living in the Now means we live in a state of bliss and beauty. We want blissfulness when in fact unblissfulness is still in us, but we don't want to acknowledge it. If we live our unblissfulness though, it will be much less unpleasant—if we really enter into and don't play evasive games.

We are not separate from Now, unless we separate ourselves. Our Now is what we feel at this moment. Five minutes from now, we might feel something different, so our Now will be different if we are in the dynamic flow of our feelings. The more truthfully we face ourselves, the more real time will be for us. This doesn't require some special time-travelling ability, we just need to learn to be present with what we think, feel and experience now.

We can start by admitting that we don't want to face our current unpleasantness, if that is what is present in the moment. Just be fully with that. This isn't something only spiritually evolved people can do—rather, it's the doorway to becoming spiritually evolved. No special gifts or stunts are required.

Ironically, since the ability to be in the present is naturally already in us, it is easier to summon the present than to go through our usual elaborate efforts to evade the Now. It's just that we have trained ourselves—over hundreds and hundreds of Earth-years—to jump out of the present moment. This is actually quite a feat that is a much more difficult procedure than being with what is.

So where do we start? Awareness is always the first step. Once we see that we do indeed struggle away from the Now, we'll realize that we haven't yet found the reason why. Our investigation will give us an inkling about it, but we must realize there's also an opposite side to this conflict: we also fear this future we are striving for, whose hallmarks are death and decay.

So we are simultaneously straining toward the future while we want to stop the movement of time and even go backwards into our youth. Needless to say, the soul suffers from tension when it gets caught in this useless tug-of-war that wastes so much energy.

Fear of death opposes the natural movement of time, which is steady and harmonious. If we can feel into this rhythm, we can come into harmony with it. And even though we may not yet be in the highest state of be-ing, we will be in a state of being which is a match for the dimension of time we are in. Then we just follow the flow. This wave will carry us natu-rally and gracefully to the next dimension of time—the one we fear so much because we can't prove it is real.

Our haste, on the one hand, to get into the new dimension, smacks up against our fear of the unknown, sending our soul into opposite direc-tions. The result? Stagnation of growth and more veering away from the fullness of Now.

If we can locate this tugging in diametrically opposing directions, we may be motivated to unearth the nature of it. What particular functions in our life could stand to be improved? If we jot down notes about our inner experiences throughout the day, we'll start to make recognitions that can lead to reigniting our full spark of aliveness. That the recognitions may be unflattering and disillusioning—maybe even painful—won't diminish the great experience of dynamic peace that follows. On the contrary, it might prove the truth in these teachings.

If self-confrontation does not, in the end, lead to an uplifting experi-ence, we are not yet at the end. Don't get impatient or tense, but rather notice that somewhere, somehow, we're hedging the truth. When this happens, we're just not wanting to see all there is to see.

Why does it happen that after a painful or unflattering awareness—provided we go all the way to its depths and don't stop halfway—we ex-perience such a state of aliveness and harmony? It's because in that moment, we have fully used the fragment of time at our disposal. When-ever we feel listless or depressed, the material is right there in front of us, overlooked; we're smack dab in the middle of it but we are blind to it. We don't focus our attention on it—we merely try to get out of this Now without using it. That's the forward movement that pushes us pell-mell into our fear of death.

So if we want to experience an uninterrupted flow of time that leads in-to extended dimensions, we have to use each moment as described. Then we're not talking about concepts we might accept or reject, agree or disa-gree with. We'll have our own inner experience of realizing that the present matrix of time is just one fragment of another greater matrix.

Glimpsing this will, in itself, bring the knowledge that death is but an illusion; it's a transition into a different dimension.

#112 Humanity's Relationship to Time

PEARLS

7

Basking in Grace
& Not Building on Deficit

There was a time when grace was understood to be a special dispensation from God that was given—or not. He had his reasons, or so people believed, and we had little say in the matter. People then had very little self-responsibility, so this way of interpreting grace was acceptable.

Today, we've come a long way in the area of self-responsibility. We understand that, for better or for worse, we create our experiences and also our reality. So then where does grace come in? Has it been totally eliminated? Thankfully, no, it has not. Grace is as alive and well in self-creation and self-responsibility as ever; these are not mutually exclusive concepts. Let's go deeper in our understanding of grace and see how it also ties to faith.

For starters, the grace of God simply is. It exists all the time, all around us, penetrating everything that is. It is part of the fabric of reality, which by the way is utterly gentle, caring and kind—totally benign. Grace means that everything, in the end, will work out for the best, no matter how painfully tragic things may seem at the moment. Perhaps we've discovered this truth in our personal self-development: whenever we fully work through a negative experience, we come full circle to seeing the light of truth, love and peace—the joy of eternal life—in all ways. Therein lies grace.

So in truth, we can't help but live in God's grace. The very air we breathe is permeated with it. It's everywhere, in every substance of life, on all levels—from the crudest matter to the finest vibrations. Our entire world—the whole universe we're part of—and the divine laws that govern it are all expressions of grace. It's impossible to describe the tenderness and personal care of the living God who is an eternal presence in all that is. We live and move in it, and since we're surrounded by grace, there is simply never anything to fear—no matter how things appear right now.

The problem isn't that we need to draw God's grace to us; it's already there in every pore of our being. The problem is our faulty outlook, our limited view of things, our distorted perceptions. These are like walls of iron that wrap around us and prevent us from experiencing grace. In reality, these walls are made of mist that dissolves the moment we rearrange our field of vision—the moment we clear up our blocks and personal defects.

We begin this process by looking at our minor, everyday events. We only need to ask 'how do I feel?' That gauge is always right there at our fingertips, letting us know if we are operating in harmony with life—feeling joyous and hopeful. If so, we're bathing in God's grace that permeates us and we're in truth regarding what's happening in our world.

But when that's not the case and we are feeling disturbed, afraid—in any kind of disharmony within ourselves, with others, or with life in general—then we've forgotten the all-important key. The key is to know that when we're unhappy, fearful, discouraged or in darkness in any way, we're not in truth. If we at least know that, we will now know a smidge of truth. And that makes all the difference.

It is our blocks and our faulty vision that separate us from the grace of God, but we think it's the other way around. We put effect before cause and get confused, thinking grace is something that must be given to us. We also assume that faith comes to us from the outside, as if one day we might have it, while for now we lack it. Truth is, we lack neither grace nor faith; we're swimming in both but don't realize it. We already possess the states of consciousness we are hoping to attain.

So our work to grow, expand and develop—these all mean essentially one thing: to bring out the perfection that already exists inside of us. Thinking in these terms—that we need to release something that already exists, rather than become something we are not—can help everything to start falling into place.

"Becoming" implies we need to acquire something, as though we think we're an empty vessel that needs to be filled. But in reality, we're already *all that*, on another level of reality. Whatever we wish to be just needs to be brought out on this material level. The fact that we struggle to do this is why we have a Lower Self. Again, not the other way around.

So we can bring forward our intrinsic awareness of grace. We can release our faith—our existing inner knowing—that we live in a tender universe shaped from God's care for us. There is nothing to fear; all fear is an illusion. Seeing things in this light may surprise us, filling us with wonder and joy. Gee, why wouldn't everyone jump on this bandwagon?

The first obstacle is that we don't know that we have faith. We have to cultivate this awareness, this knowledge. We need to engage our brains in this. If we start to realize that we live in a benign world in which we're continually infused with God's grace, we'll start to challenge our fears, our doubts, our distrust. This will help give us the courage to risk giving—a vitally important lever that operates according to the laws of life. For only as we give out, from our heart, can we truly receive.

All religious scriptures of any kind teach the law of giving and receiving, but often it is slightly misunderstood so we put it aside. We think it's a sanctimonious edict that an arbitrary authority issues forth, demanding we do something so that rewards will possibly be given in return. It's like a form of bargaining. Of course we resist this—it offends our human dignity. We distrust a universe that treats us like we're unruly children.

So then what is the law of giving and receiving really about? Each of us have a built-in mechanism that makes it impossible to receive when we withhold our innate capacity and desire to give. Since, in reality, giving and receiving are one and the same movement, one can't exist without the other. This means that if we let our distrust and fear hold us back, the grace of God can't flow out.

It's like the riches are right there, but our hand can't reach for them. Our senses can't smell them or taste them or feel them; it's as though our perceptions are so dulled that our whole outlook on life is distorted. This creates the illusion that we live in a poor and empty universe. Our brains then believe that our inner universe is equally poor and empty, that we have nothing to give from and there's nothing to receive. Ooof.

The illusion that we live in an empty universe and are impoverished automatically creates vicious circles. This erroneous belief then makes us hoard ourselves, holding back our talents, our riches—everything we possess spiritually or materially. We hold in rather than give out. This is how we separate ourselves from the riches that surround us. It is our own inner mechanism that makes receiving downright impossible, seemingly confirming that 'Yep, I knew it, it's a hard-knock life.'

Alternatively, believing in truthful concepts would create harmless, happy circles. We can create these by taking the risk to give, consciously expecting that abundance will grow since fear of poverty and deprivation are illusory. If we give to God in trust and with faith, we release our inner faith and clear up our inner vision. We'll be able to see the abundance surrounding us and flowing through us, lifting the lever that locked the mechanism.

When we risk giving out, we engage a benign circle so that we can then afford to release more of our inner and outer riches. We will know that they are forever replenished by a never-ending stream. The more we receive, the more we can give, and the more we give, the more we are capable of receiving. That's when giving and receiving become one.

There's an obstacle many face in establishing a happy circle of abundance that's in harmony with divine grace and divine order. This is an important aspect to consider as it exists on every level—inner and outer, emotional and psychological, personal and collective. It's the tendency for people to build on deficit. This is intrinsically linked to this belief in an empty, poor, ungiving world.

Whenever we stack positive beliefs on top of negative ones we are only half-aware of, we are building on deficit. So if we secretly believe we are unlovable or unacceptable, despite our surface behaviors to the contrary, we're building on deficit. When we hold onto guilt—real or false, doesn't matter—that stops us from giving ourselves over to God, we're building on deficit. When we assume this world is a hostile place and set about protecting ourselves with destructive defenses—whether we know we're doing this or not—we're building on deficit.

The trouble with building on deficit is that it appears to work, at least for a while. It's temporarily convincing. We could, for example, build a lovely-looking house on sandy ground. It would hold up for awhile, but when it starts to crumble, the builder won't remember the decision to build on such a weak foundation. The cracks in the walls will later be ascribed to some other cause, with rationalizations used to maintain the illusion and encourage more building on deficit.

Walking a spiritual path of self-discovery is intended to expose all the deficits that we ignore. Painful as this may be at first, it is the way to create inner order so we can begin to build on real assets. We never want our "inner economics" to become fraudulent or unsound. The temporary pain we feel at being exposed is caused by our wrong conclusion that we are now doomed to accept the "reality" of our poverty.

We keep running on empty, giving out in a distorted way that has nothing to do with genuine giving. We don't trust that we can create riches based on a healthy concept about life. We pretend to give whenever we face the world wearing a mask while we inwardly despair about who we really are. We give as a way to manipulate others so we will get what we don't believe we deserve. This is how the Lower Self gives, and it amounts to building on deficit.

These false ways may work for a bit, but as the deficit piles up, we must work harder to cover up our impoverishment if we hope to avoid bankruptcy. We grab at unsound means to keep the pretense going, cherishing the illusion that we can go on this way indefinitely.

We also buy into the mistaken Lower-Self belief that the world is mean and poor. The upshot of all this is that we only believe in illusory wealth acquired by scheming, greed and trickery. We don't believe in the real wealth of God's creation.

With this as the foundation we are standing on, pouring our energy into our mask and our Lower Self, we don't dare to expose our deficits—the inner bankruptcy that smolders underneath. This is why a path of spiritual purification is about bringing out all of our guilts and all of our Lower

Self maneuvers. We must stand there poor, no longer covered up with a fake veneer.

We need to stop avoiding the poverty we have unwittingly created through our false beliefs and our destructive means. These only work to increase the deficit. We need to look at our fear of declaring bankruptcy which we resist and cover up, and which we can finally overcome through our faith. Then we can start building real inner wealth on sound footings.

Any personal crisis is nothing more than a bankruptcy exposed. We can wait for this to happen on its own, or we can create a controlled fall by working mindfully with a spiritual helper or counselor. By going through the shame of revealing our deficits, we stop building on them. We can then sail through the fear and pain of believing this is our final reality—the truth of who we are. This is how we must go if we want to discover the real wealth behind our frantic efforts to hide our poverty. We must stop pretending in a false wealth and building on deficit.

Of course our spiritual and emotional "finances" appear on the physical level as well. We often live above our means, coasting on debt and covering one hole with another newly created hole. This creates anxiety but we don't attempt to create order instead, believing as we do that order and abundance don't exist for us. Perhaps we're not willing to give our best to our work, so we don't make a decent living. We depend on others and accumulate debt. We run from creating a budget that could help to establish order.

These same patterns of finances and economics are also followed collectively by governments, where we could build on assets and reserves instead of debts and emptiness. Whenever a country goes through some kind of severe crisis—such as riots, revolutions, war or financial collapse—it has waited too long to establish order by making deliberate good choices. It's the result of not wanting to expose the deficits so that true abundance could be established. It's not so different from an individual meltdown that happens when someone refuses to expose their inner pretenses and poverty.

Governments can also create spiritual deficit when they scheme and lie to deceive people, promote injustice, and operate on drives for greed and power. Such imbalances can only go on for so long; they must surface so that a new order can be established. Going through such a crisis will often result in changes made with the best intentions. New laws and ways of operating will emerge along with possibly new forms of government.

But then the inner meaning gets lost again and the forces of darkness tempt people by distorting the truth; the same deficit rises up through different means. So the solution never lies in the form of government we adopt or the outer measures we collectively institute, even though some measures may admittedly be better than others at times.

Taking a hard and well-informed look at a government will reveal where and how their deficits get created. We can see how they coast along on debt, never believing that real wealth can be established. It's too frightening for them to admit the imbalance and mismanagement. There's no faith in the possibility of an honest picture so they settle for a false world picture of a poor, empty, untrustworthy universe.

Taking a step into faith is only possible by going to and with God. Risking to have faith is how we create faith—by then experiencing that faith is justified. So it's foolish for us to think we can create an abundant, harmonious government in which peace and justice prevail without having a direct communication with the Christ that permeates all that is.

If we ignore God, we can't perceive his presence or hear his guidance and inspiration. Then we can't summon the courage we need to expose our temporary bankruptcy. This is as true for countries as for couples and for individuals. Then the shambles can be collected and the structure rebuilt in a better way. This is the hope for the world we live in.

Whatever we undertake without God, no matter how smart and efficient, is bound to fail in the long run. But with God, we can find the courage and honesty to have total openness. Then we can rebuild in earnest and in glory. Only in this way will any government be able to run on assets with a healthy flow of giving and receiving, never exhausting its reserves.

Nothing in this world ever happens by accident, and there is no wisdom from the creator that doesn't have deep reasoning and meaning. So consider why God distributed our world's resources so that some are in certain parts only and others are in other parts. It is so that countries will learn to not deny other countries their resources. Then power plays won't corrupt this world that God created in which all can partake of everything, regardless of its origin. People will learn to share and consider *all* people.

This will allow people and societies to freely receive what they need and that others have to give. So countries must learn to share their resources, not hoard them or deprive people of them as a way to gain more power and riches.

As we work to restore balance in our spiritual communities and personal situations, here are some guiding principles we can follow.

- Consider whether it is more appropriate for the individual to be giving to the collective entity, or whether this process should be reversed and the whole can give more to support a part.

- We shouldn't live beyond our means. Function from fullness instead of running on deficit. Have faith and establish priorities. Know that on the material level, it may sometimes be unavoidable to avoid debt until it is possible to function on assets. We may need to keep our budget smaller than we wish or temporarily do without something essential until we can afford it. Reconsider what really is and is not essential.

- Know that we may have to temporarily pitch in more with our giving to build something substantial. None will come to deprivation from their giving; to the contrary, more abundance will accrue. This will allow more to give individually so that individuals can then receive from a healthy collective.

Often we need to tackle a problem from both sides. We need to expose and purify what runs on deficit as we work to create a budget and live in balance and harmony. This is the way to true abundance that is well earned, honestly deserved and can therefore be guiltlessly enjoyed. Our first step is to risk giving out.

Then we must consider that the fear that causes us to hold and hoard is in error. Giving through faith—even before we're convinced that our fear of giving is unfounded—is like pulling out poisonous weeds and planting beautiful seedlings instead. This is the way to create a fertile, rich spiritual garden—a real, tangible thing—to enjoy now and not in some faraway dream only realizable in the afterlife.

We need to recognize the divine laws and principles at work here. We also need to recognize whatever obstructs us from partaking of ever-present divine grace. Then we can release the faith that is in us, not as an act of blind belief in wishful thinking but as a new ground rule for life.

#250 Inner Awareness of Grace—Exposing the Deficit

8

Articulating the Power of the Word

This work of spiritual transformation is a magnificent process. Through it we are literally reintegrating split off parts of ourselves which, when left on their own, create and recreate painful patterns. Over time, these aspects generate momentum resulting in negative patterns that carry the day; we get caught in them and can't reverse them. We seem to be their victim and no longer connect with how we created this movement we're carried in.

But it is possible to unwind all this, to reverse the momentum and rise up from the charred remains of our faulty creations. Let's look at precisely how such a process can be consciously initiated to transition from negative creations to positive self-perpetuating motion, all by using our voluntary will and the power of the word. Yes, we can do this.

Exactly what is the word? It is the creative agent that launches movement and a systematic chain reaction, with one link inexorably following another. By the end of the line, the word becomes a deed, a fact—a finished creation.

Words are the blueprint necessary for building any structure. The word, in fact, is what's behind all creation; nothing in creation can exist unless a word has been spoken, known, held, believed in and committed to. The word both expresses and creates by forming patterns of energy that then form additional nucleuses where each point or link—which are also words—becomes a secondary creative agent. The word is plan and opinion, knowledge and consciousness, feeling and attitude and intention. Words carry their own kind of powerful energy that is not like other energies. Words are all this and more.

The spoken word reveals the will—either divine will or the split off ignorant will—that is the motivating force behind what is being uttered. In any area where we speak, our words are the sum total of our beliefs, be they conscious or not. Like the sun that creates the planets, the word is the energizing force and it is the design. So incredibly much is contained within the word.

Holy Scripture starts by postulating that in the beginning was—or actually *is*—the word. The word is eternal; it will always be. It is from God's spoken word that all creation came into being, including our personalities. It's behind the creation of everything from our unique feelings and experiences to planetary systems and the greater consciousness of all people.

So what do we do with this truth? How can we put it to good use in our daily lives? Well, for one thing, we can become aware that every situation we experience in life is the product of words we ourselves have spoken. Day in and day out, in every hour and every minute, we are constantly speaking words on various levels of our being. The goal of this spiritual path is to make all these words conscious, because that is the only way for us to understand our creations.

Unfortunately, we spend a lot of time busily blocking out the words we speak. We actually produce inner noise for this very purpose. Just what is it we're saying that we don't wish to hear?

Words can be in disagreement within themselves. This happens when we speak opposite words on different levels of our awareness so that they effectively cancel each other out. This confuses us and we create accordingly. We also create fog so that we can't see what we're saying, allowing some words to overshadow others. We need to get clear about which words are doing the creating, especially of the stuff we don't like. These are sharp tools we're handling; it's time to see the power they wield to produce disasters or delightful successes.

When we speak words of beauty and truth, but underneath lies incompatible material, we create at best a short circuit and at worst a split in our consciousness. This is why it's preferable in the beginning to honestly admit the negativity of our Lower Self. This is an act of truthfulness, humility, courage and faith, and there's nothing wrong with these Higher Self qualities.

If, on the other hand, we speak words that reveal divine principles but do so while the Lower Self is still hidden, we're standing in a line-up of wishful thinking, pride, lack of faith and a fear of letting others see our imperfections. We're shirking the process of growing and healing in a realistic way. Words about limitless abundance, then, can be spoken without being in truth.

There is a direct link between the words we choose and our self-value. Think about it: is it possible to talk about faith and the unfoldment of our beings from one side of our mouths, while we're silently whispering that we have no value from the other? Deep in our hearts, we all carry some shards of feeling worthless; how can we challenge this if we secretly are terrified that worthlessness is the truth of who we are? All we can do is to block this "knowledge" and defend ourselves against it.

In truth, it's these defensive maneuvers that reinforce this notion that we're unacceptable. This is so because our defenses are purely destructive guilt-generators. So even if we become belligerent and tell ourselves we do deserve peace of mind, pleasure and abundance, deep down we feel we don't really deserve this and so fear we'll never have it.

Worse, we fear that if we did manage any kind of fulfillment, we'd need to steal it and would therefore be punished. So on the surface we may speak words about what we long for—which is the same as what every human longs for and indeed should experience—while simultaneously cutting ourselves off at the knees on another level. This state of division and self-denial makes us pessimistic about life and fearful of the world. Our vision is fragmented and so is our experience.

Our goal: establish a one-pointed word. It will take honesty and courage to expose ourselves and our devastating belief in our lack of value. We must pierce through our facades and cover-up stories to see our painful feelings about being unlovable, and then cast our doubt on our self-doubt. This is the avenue that leads to pronouncements of real truth.

We can pry open the lid of our self-doubt with questions about the truth. "Is it true that I need to defend myself to feel my value?" "Under my arrogance, am I floundering in doubt about my value?" Then we can ask ourselves: "Is it true my faults make me undeserving and unlovable?" "Is there something in me that justifies loving myself?" Such questions can carry words of truth.

Words are no less powerful when they are not articulated well. Vague and hazy words need to be crystallized and brought out from behind the smoke screen. Start to see the energy that thoughts hold and the power they have to create. This is not the same energy as is expressed on other levels, since the mental, physical, emotional and will levels each express in different ways. Just don't underestimate the power and energy of the word.

We may think our thoughts and comments—either said loudly or silently—do not matter. So not true. The silent word is not necessarily less powerful than a word that is uttered. In fact, words that wash across our vocal chords may well have much less energy than the ones held inside that are rooted in strong beliefs. We use these lightly spoken words, said without feeling or conviction, to fill the void inside us with fog. This separates our consciousness from the words we speak that do have power—for good or for bad—and therefore this pitter-patter of thoughts has a serious effect.

We are the ones who wittingly or unwittingly set the creative process in motion—through *all* our words. By tuning into the underground noise, and observing and identifying our words, we will gain a much better understanding of how we create our lives.

Sometimes our words contradict divine truth, sending our energies into involuntary patterns that make life seem dangerous and foreign. It feels like we must defend ourselves against life, like we're a helpless pawn. So we can pick another word that aligns with the truth of creation and start creating benign circles of love and bliss, joy and abundance.

No joy? No abundance? We must be speaking a word that denies this possibility. Maybe we secretly believe we don't deserve it. Maybe we don't think it even exists. Perhaps we feel too bad or evil to deserve fulfillment. All this might be hidden from our conscious mind, which generally just feels pessimistic and adrift. Then feelings of helplessness may seem overwhelming. Know this: there is a chain of cause and effect linking our words and our experience. It can be found and unkinked.

Holding onto a nihilistic belief about a terrible world may seem preferable to seeing our own painful belief that we're not worthy of the joy of life. But folks, if we believe this, we're not in truth. We need to find the words behind such thoughts. Find the ones that say 'it's dangerous to love, it will hurt me.' These are untruths that create nothing but painful patterns that make them seem true. But no, still not truth. These words—not real reality—are what keep us from experiencing the fulfillment we long for.

Some words are spoken so deep in our unconscious we're not at all aware of them. It's like they're spoken at the bottom of the ocean while we're splashing around on the surface. But with one ear under the water, we can start to tune into them. This is the kind of effort we must make to dredge them up, following whatever hints and clues we notice. Sitting quietly in meditation is a good opportunity to listen.

We're referring here to "words" rather than "thoughts" because the word is what immediately creates; it's the energy explosion. The thought is the content—the result of underlying factors—that goes on to express itself through the word. That said, the word occurs at the inception of the thought, so it's not possible to have a thought without the word. It simply could not exist. But again, the word may or may not occur at the level of our conscious awareness or be vocalized.

The main take-away here is this: we need to take care with our words, making space for them to become clear and taking responsibility for the words we say quietly within. We can question their origin: do they arise from a truthful thought or an untruthful one? We can reject, revise and debate our thoughts before the word clinches them, forming the finished product of the thought and beginning to create.

Differentiating between words and thoughts may seem like we're splitting hairs, but it's not. If, for example, we feel unworthy of the best life has to offer, we can question this thought. But if we speak these words within ourselves, it's a creation that we now take for granted. It doesn't occur to us to challenge it, debate it and therefore correct it. That's how, unaware to us, we're giving such a thought power.

The boat of our lives rocks back and forth over this kind of undercurrent, which carries us to unfortunate destinations. Not only do we no longer notice the current, we no longer see how we created it and can change it. Anywhere we notice that our creations are limited and undesirable, we must look for the associated words that are responsible and begin to say different ones.

If we do this by way of a superficial mantra, pasting 'yes, I am worthy' over opposing words buried below, we'll create a short circuit. Then we're paying lip service in our thoughts and minds without unearthing the opposite word. We will know this is happening by looking at what's manifesting. Make no mistake, that's the pudding that always proves what's really being spoken within.

Until we unwind all this for ourselves, we may be convinced that the positive words spoken on the surface are all that count. We might then use the fact of our opposite experiences as proof that life is unfair and untrustworthy—that our own inner processes have no bearing on what goes on. People, we then think, are victims of life.

Once we go a little further in our work though, we will uncover our unfortunate self-hate and our lack of faith in our own Higher Self. Knowing this information about words will help in our search for the imposters, those parts of ourselves who still speak on our behalf but don't represent our best interest.

There are two words—giving and receiving—that deep inside ourselves sound like opposites, and this misnomer creates a crazy-big conflict. Mentally, superficially, we may have gotten the message that giving and receiving are one and the same thing. But many of us haven't experienced this truth yet. So emotionally, there may be quite the chasm between them.

Here's how this goes. When we knock our own value through the words we say to ourselves, we become afraid. Our fear makes us avoid moving out into the world so our heart won't flow into another's. We think the ticket out of this miserable state is to be loved. So then along comes love, but no matter how much we long for it, we can't let it in; we find excuses to not accept it. Our mind may be divided but the truth that giving and receiving are one is still evident: as we don't give, so we can't receive.

To take in love, we must feel we are worthy of it. But if we feel worthless, then being loved threatens to expose this pain. Giving love also suffers, because we can only give love when we feel we deserve the pleasure of doing so. So to receive love, we must feel we deserve it, and that can't happen if we don't wish to love. Anyone else feeling dizzy?

It's a false idea that if we were loved, we could then love. This simply doesn't work. These are false words we speak into ourselves on some level. No one else can give us the love and sense of worth we need to give to ourselves. Often, in fact, we are given to, but we reject what comes in the form of sincere love—from others, from God and from life itself.

Due to our wrong thinking, we experience an impossible division—we can't receive because we don't give—instead of the oneness of giving and receiving. For in the simple act of taking in love, we are giving; not being willing to take in what is given is a form of ungivingness. So taking is already giving, as long as we're not grabbing or cheating. We can experience this in the way it hurts when something we have to give another is not wanted. But when they receive from us, they give us something.

All this can become an endless flow, even though we may sometimes find ourselves more in one stage, perhaps giving only through our sincere receiving. That's all right. If we receive in truth and beauty, we'll become stronger in other kinds of giving, including giving from our resources. We just need to articulate the appropriate words to ourselves. These are the ones that support our growing power to give and receive, each in truth, wisdom, beauty and alignment with God's will.

It takes courage to speak words of truth such as 'I can give my best and let God give through me—in truth, wisdom, beauty, strength and sincerity.' For one thing, we'll need to give up our misguided safety nets, including our shaky conclusions about the negative nature of life. *And darn it, we've invested so much into this.* But unless such falsehoods are relinquished, true words can't be said.

We'll need to have faith in a kind and caring universe, and such faith, in turn, requires a commitment. We must extend ourselves into unexplored alternatives, believing in a possibility we haven't yet experienced for ourselves. Having the courage to pronounce words of truth is the prerequisite to knowing a new truth. And faith, in the end, is always made up of courage and strength. Truer words were never said.

#233 The Power of the Word

9

Why Flubbing on Perfection
is the Way to Find Joy

What does it mean to "find God?" Is that even a real thing? And if it happened, what would that look like? Would it make us perfect?

For real, there is such a thing as finding God, and there's nothing hazy or unrealistic about it. It's actually a very concrete process and—*oh, happy day!*—yields tangible results. When we find God, we understand the laws of the universe—we get how the world works—and we are capable of loving and relating. We experience joy and are truly self-responsible. We have integrity and the courage to be ourselves, even if that means giving up someone else's approval. All this is what happens when we find God. Well that's funny—this looks exactly like what happens when we find our true selves. Finding God then, by whatever name we call the process, is the same as finding ourselves—coming home from self-alienation.

A built-in aspect of finding of our honest-to-goodness real selves includes having the capacity to feel joy and to give joy. But dang it, we can't give what we don't have, and just how are we to become joyful when we live in such an imperfect world?

Whether we realize it or not, we associate a joyful life with a perfect one. We can't enjoy life if we're not perfect—or so we think—nor can we enjoy our neighbors or our lovers or our situation in life. So let's pause right here because this is one of humanity's biggest bonehead beliefs.

Sure, we know in our heads there is no perfection in this life. That's why we repress our inner reaction to imperfect situations. But our repression causes the conflict—and our confusion about it—to go up and not down. So there is a discrepancy between what's in our heads and what happens in our emotions. Essentially, we demand perfection, and that's just not what's happening.

It's time to connect the dots between how our need for perfection alienates us from our true selves, which in turn hoses up our chances for a joyful life. No one's shooting unrealistically for 100% joy here, but it could be possible to have a lot more joy than we do now.

Odd as this may seem, our capacity to give and receive joy is linked with our acceptance of imperfection—not in theory but in our gut-level emotions. These, of course, are two entirely different animals. We can start by accepting that we have this discrepancy inside ourselves, which takes a great deal of systematic self-search to do for even a moment.

Only by accepting an imperfect relationship—and this doesn't mean submitting in an unhealthy way because we fear being alone or disapproved of—will we get and give joy in the relationship. And only by accepting that we are imperfect beings can we grow out of our imperfections and enjoy the experience of being who we really are, right now. We need to stop being out of touch with reality as we know it.

Many of us have become so good at repressing our feelings that we're not fully aware of our own unfulfillment, of our frustrations. We know perfection can't be had so we vaguely skip over what falls short of perfection. But our effort to remain unaware of what we're feeling generates a lot of destructive energy.

Two things are harmful about this repression. First, had we chosen awareness instead, we could have seen how our frustration was uncalled-for; we could have looked at the patterns responsible for our frustration and done something about them. Second, when we're busy repressing, we're not in position to accept what we can't change—namely, that life and people are imperfect. Doh.

We need a certain level of awareness to discriminate between what we should change—in order to have more fulfillment—and to know when we're rolling over because it's just easier that way. Deep down, we're often pitching a hissy fit over whatever is unchangeable while at the same time, our impossible demand for perfection causes us to stagnate—we won't change our inner patterns, which could lead to so much more fulfillment.

Step one for finding our way out of this paper bag we're lost in is to give ourselves the luxury of facing our longings. What do we desire and what's our complaint against life or fate or others for not having it? If we resent that something in our lives isn't perfect, we need to come face-to-face with our resentment. Only if we fully face our resentment against imperfection can we begin to accept imperfection. And only by accepting imperfection can we find enjoyment in our relationships and in life.

Continually striving for perfection though—and remember, perfection doesn't even exist here on Earth—keeps us from accepting what truly is. That's how we spoil our lives and our relationships. It keeps us from growing and thus changing whatever needs to be changed and made better—even though it's never going to be perfect.

This may seem like a paradox: we are only capable of joy if we accept imperfection; to grow, we must accept our own imperfections. But if we think about it, this makes sense. And really, how hard could it be? In practice, it is often very difficult because we're not aware of our own feelings and reactions. We have so many hidden crevices inside ourselves, it will require our full attention to peer into them. Good news, once we've made some progress, it will become super-cinchy to do this because we'll be staring at the truth.

And what's the truth again? That this world is imperfect. That's reality. What's the reality, or truth, of the current state of our soul? We don't accept imperfection. We need to face the reality of both of these truths—one about the world and the other about the state of our soul.

Those who are actively engaged in doing this work of self-development often get tripped up by perfectionistic attitudes toward themselves: "I should have worked through my problems by now. I can't be happy until my problems are resolved, so I must be impatient, compulsive and restless. I can't live in the imperfect present but must always be living in the future when I hope to be perfect. Then I'll experience perfect happiness, perfect love and perfect relationships."

Of course, we don't formulate such thoughts so clearly. But if we could translate our emotions, this is how they would sound. Then it dawns on us that we're never going to get there—we'll never resolve all our issues in this lifetime. This makes us discouraged: "Why bother? Why face all these truths inside myself?" This kind of reaction typifies a perfectionistic attitude about spiritual growth. Unconsciously, we're planning to go the route of achieving complete perfection. None of this step-by-step growth business for us.

People, we don't have to be problem-free. In truth, we cannot be. We don't have to be perfect to live fully, have more awareness and enjoy more fulfilling experiences. Accepting our imperfections, in fact, makes us less imperfect and flexible enough to change. It's our haste and shame about not being perfect that create rigid walls, obliterating the possibility for change.

The trouble, as is often the case, is our dualistic either/or attitude. Either we strive for immediate perfection—ignoring what's still not perfect—or we give up. We think that if we accept that we're not perfect, we'll get stuck there. This is one coin with two sides, and neither is in truth. If we let both go, we can discover the healthy productive approach.

Another aspect of our wrong attitude of perfectionism is that we think—not consciously, but below in our unconscious mind—that we must meet a standard imposed on us by an outer authority—by rules, by religion, by the world. Hence our efforts to become perfect, be they ever so subtle, lead us from away from ourselves. We need to connect with the goals of our true self. What do *we* feel and want and fear?

If we focus on growing—rather than on being perfect—we'll live in the Now. We'll find our own values and let go of those we've taken on from the outside. We'll do what we do for our own sake and not for the sake of appearances. Finding our own values leads us back to ourselves—away from self-alienation; that's the way to find harmony within. This will anchor us in ourselves.

We may be quick to respond with 'Oh no, I don't pretend. I don't do anything for appearance's sake.' We need to look for this on the level of our emotions, not our minds. Not one human being is entirely free from this. If we can accept this imperfection in us, we can grow. Not accepting our perfectionism stunts our growth.

We're so conditioned to manipulating our emotions it may take considerable effort to see how we do it. Given our perfectionism, we recognize that some of our conscious feelings aren't, well, all that perfect, so we superimpose other emotions over the top of them. As such, we don't function naturally or organically, so how can we be our real selves? In the beginning, it will be a chore just to see how unnatural we are.

In our natural state, our real self will always dare to be spontaneous. But spontaneity is out of the question if we're hampering our feelings. Examples of how we tamper with our feelings include being overly emotional, overly dramatic, exaggerating our feelings, and talking ourselves into stronger feelings than we actually have. It is not harmless that we do these things that are so self-alienating.

Here's something else we do to blunt the full force of our feelings: we couple a wrong kind of caution—a fearful holding back—with a forceful will—a pushy forcing current. Both ways are often adopted by the same person. Over-dramatizing is connected with using power as our defensive strategy. Repressing feelings is connected with withdrawing, escaping and pretending we are more serene than we are.

Offhand, it might seem like exaggerating feelings makes them stronger, but anything that is not genuine leads to self-alienation and therefore shallowness. When we're over-emotional, we wish to bend life and people to meet our needs. That is a true manipulation.

The forcing current originates from the urgency caused by unmet needs. The more unaware we are of our needs, the more we repress them and the more forceful will be the urge for fulfillment. What we need to do is become aware of our needs and understand them, and then the urgency and compulsivity will recede, which is a large part of the reason we tamper with our feelings.

The urgency of our unrecognized needs causes us to build up our emotions out of all proportion. It's like we're saying, "If my feelings are strong enough, they will be met." Or if we're of a more fearful and pessimistic character, we won't admit they exist at all. We'll ignore their urgency and squeeze our emotions out of our awareness—but not out of existence.

Making our emotions stronger or weaker cripples their functioning. Then our intuition can't unfold, nor can our creativity or spontaneity. This cuts us off from the richness of our feelings, impoverishing us. We live on the periphery of our being and feel shallow.

Our aim is to become fully aware of what we're feeling. We need to sit back and let our emotions come all the way to the surface. Note, that doesn't mean we have to act on them. Just notice them. Perceive their actual intensity and compare that with what we thought we felt before. This practice will give us a different outlook on our problems and a good sense of what it means to be our true selves.

Once we get started, we may find we only notice our reactions a few days after they happen. We might become angry with ourselves for noticing later what we "should" have noticed at the time. But note the progress. Until now, we might never have become aware of our real reaction. Delayed reaction is progress over dimmed awareness. Notice too the imperfection—we can't become perfectly aware all at once. Rejoice in the growth process and work to shorten the interval.

We need to learn to make the best of real situations because when we can't cope with reality, we're bound to make the worst of them. Then we can't get any joy from imperfect situations, which is what life is made of.

#97 Perfectionism Obstructs Happiness—Manipulation of Emotions

10

Two Rebellious
Reactions to Authority

L ife is like a school. No, that's not correct; *life is a school*. We go from one class—or incarnation—to the next, making the grade or else getting held back. The goal is to learn and grow. Knowing this, however, doesn't solve a single problem. For that, we have to understand our own unique existence. For example, why do we react to authority as we do? Most of us have a lot to learn in this respect.

We face our first conflict with authority at a very young age. Parents, siblings, relatives and later teachers all represent authority whose job is seemingly to say No. Authority then is a hostile denier of wishes. No matter how much warmth and affection is given, no matter now necessary the prohibition sometimes is, authority represents a hurdle in life.

The attitude a child has towards authority gets carried over into adulthood where unconscious reactions to authority are a good purveyor of whether the hurdles were turned into stepping stones toward maturity. When a grown-up shows they can adjust freely to authority, they are showing they have passed a milestone in their soul's development. Here's a gold star.

If, however, a person reacts childishly and compulsively to authority, there's more work to do. *Summer school, perhaps?* Up until reaching this turning point, a person will react negatively toward authority, even if it's meted out perfectly. But alas, people are imperfect which means authority is often handled in a less-than-perfect way. Lots to learn for everyone.

So there's a barrier between the child and the adult in authority. It's worse if love is lacking or not given the way child would like it, but even if the love is there, the conflict will exist. On one hand, the child wants the parent's love, and on the other, the child rebels against being restricted. Authority, then, is the hostile force of an enemy locking us behind prison bars and causing frustration.

The child then develops an impatient longing to grow up and become an adult so these restricting walls will go away. But then the child actually does grow up and the face of authority merely changes. Now, instead of parents and teachers, authority takes the form of society, the government, police officers, bosses and other people in positions of power we must now depend upon. Same conflict, different day.

Back in the days of our childhood, we were torn between wanting love and acceptance, and wanting to fight whoever who was in authority. That's a tough spot to be in that made it impossible to rebel, or so we thought. As adults, we suffer from this same basic conflict: openly rebel against restrictions or face the stigma of being ostracized and despised.

Unfortunately, the ways we usually try to resolve this don't work. Let's look at the two basic options all human beings choose from and how they are faulty. Each of the two categories overlap and have many subdivisions, and although we tend to have a favorite, we each play both ends at one time or another. For clarity, we'll explore them separately, but remember: there's always a mix.

First, let's explore those who rebel and revolt. If this is our reaction, we see authority as our enemy because many of our desires that were neither bad nor harmful—as kids or later as adults—were forbidden by someone in authority. We think 'there's nothing wrong with what I want,' yet some-one said No. Therefore we see authority as unjust and harmful, as well as narrow-minded and unhelpful.

If we feel this way and we have an extroverted nature—along with a healthy dose of chutzpah—our rebellion will be in the form of open fighting and resisting. For others, rebellion will be dimmed to a dull defiance. So this reaction can span the scale from a mild private attitude to overt social backlash to associating with an anarchy group or committing crimes. The mildest form may not be noticeable to others; the strongest form will be found in one who commits antisocial acts. But the same rebellious feelings simmer underground in either case and create outer tangible effects.

The other category includes those who, at one time or another, turned around and thought, "If I join forces with the one in authority, much as I might hate them, I will be safe." The extreme type in this category becomes the strict law-upholder, in both overt and subtle ways. It's possible there will be a strong preference for order and organization, and a desire for peace rather than fighting. In an effort to safeguard our chosen position as a law-upholder and keep our rebelliousness hidden—which deep down is no different from that of the law-breaker—we will stand in rigid opposition to the law-breaker.

The more we fear our tendency to rebel buried inside, the more we, as the law-upholder, will become severe with the law-breaker; we don't want that part of ourselves exposed that we can see in the law-breaker. In fact, fear of exposing true feelings is exactly what seems so dangerous and risky; it's why we joined the enemy camp. This fear of exposure motivates the law-upholder to be doubly "good."

In both cases, there may be true goodness within, but both are reacting ignorantly and immaturely. In the case of the law-upholder, we are acting from fear and weakness, and nothing good can ever come from that. We must make free, strong choices if we are hoping for a positive outcome.

It is a truth that the unconscious of one person has an infinitely stronger effect on another's unconscious than any surface action or motive ever could. So an act driven by fear will impact someone else more strongly than the same act carried out with a clear recognition of our own inner tendencies. This means that the law-upholder—with their wrong motivations—will have a particularly bad effect on the law-breaker. The more hidden the forces, the more adverse the effect.

Note, the reaction will be quite different—much less rebellious— toward a law-upholder who has healthy, mature motives based on strength instead of weakness. It should also be noted that all of this reference to "law-upholders" and "law-breakers" applies in a psychological sense, not only in reference to social laws that everyone is expected to abide.

We humans have a habit of learning that one tendency is wrong, which makes us swing over to the other equally wrong extreme. We need to stop doing this. So don't misunderstand and conclude that the stance of the law-breaker is more desirable simply because the opposite is also imperfect.

Here's how these two opposite extremes hook each other in a vicious circle. The bigger the rebellion on the part of the law-breaker, the more intolerant and severe the law-upholder becomes; the latter is trying to protect themselves from their own fear and rebellion. This makes the resistance and rebellion of the law-breaker even greater. The law-breaker isn't aware of the fact that they're no longer fighting against the law, as such, or even against the good and true aspect of authority. They are turned against the false notes of goody-goodyness coming from the equally unaware law-upholder. And so we go round the mulberry bush.

This is a subtle subject, but if we examine our lives it won't be too hard to figure out which camp we're mostly in. So then what's the remedy? If we're the revolter type, we can meditate on the divine qualities of real authority and how that differs from the imperfect human variety. Perhaps we can only see the distorted version; maybe we've never encountered a true authority. Just seeing this can lessen our resistance. Then we won't mind half as much when the imperfect provider of true laws and authority appears, which is as much for our protection as for anyone else's. It won't feel like an enemy force.

This is the way to build a proper concept about authority, so we can sense the wrong kind and not be so reactionary. We'll see how currents in the "enemy" are also in us, just manifesting differently. This is the process for raising our level of consciousness—our maturity. Then we'll be able to see the need for law and order, and appreciate the task of the authorities who are there to uphold it. OK, so maybe the ideal of this principle does not abound on planet Earth. Yet. But we still need whatever we currently have. And we need to get our rebellion in check.

As more of us do the work of self-development, we will step more and more into our own authority—although not necessarily on a particular subject. Perhaps we've come across someone like this who is very good and wise and kind, without being perfect. Emanations from such a person are not the same as those coming from a law-upholder who is motivated by weakness and fear. But unless we do our own work, we won't be able to intuitively recognize someone like this, and instead we'll react automatically against them just because they represent authority. We are blinded by our own rigid intention to revolt.

Once we become aware of these two different kinds of authority—the self-righteous kind and the true essence—we can divorce ourselves from our knee-jerk reaction of rejecting all authority. This is how to use our healthy reasoning process to learn to have sound discernment—not just intellectually, but also intuitively.

For people in the law-abider bucket, it may be helpful to search childhood memories to find the times when we revolted. This will help to uncover the memories of when we decided to turn around and jump ship. Sure, there were good motives in doing so, but also weak ones. Search for both. This will shed light on the reaction others have to us; this will loosen the stranglehold on our self-righteous severity towards our brothers and sisters. We will, of course, remain on the side of the law, as we should— both inner law and outer law—but with a softer approach. In this, we will find compassion for the law-breaker so we can help them out of their brand of error.

This explanation about our reaction to authority sheds lights on why Jesus brought so much censure upon himself. He regularly associated with lowly people—common criminals and prostitutes—who didn't rebel against Jesus because they could sense his true goodness and his understanding of them. Jesus didn't judge them but instead went with them, in spite of his being opposed to their wrong acts or attitudes. He could even laugh with them, and also laugh at the wrong kind of pompous authority that is so proud of itself.

Jesus showed us the kind of authority to strive for. We can build common ground with others by seeing how their reaction lives in us, but not setting ourselves up as the judge. This balance is tricky to attain; we can only find it through solving our own inner struggle against authority.

None of this means we shouldn't punish law-breakers; that would be missing the point. When we're at the stage of being dangerous to others, we have to learn a lesson. But when things get this far advanced, we can be sure that the wrong kind of authority prevailed too long. The effects of discipline from authority have driven the law-breaker into deeper ignorance and darkness, instead of lifting them out of it.

All our miseries—criminal behavior, wars, diseases and injustices of any kind—are really the result of long-standing faults. So the remedy may not be quick or easy. A whole chain reaction has to be painstakingly unwound to get to the roots of the problem. There we will find a raging vicious circle that has to be clearly understood. Certainly, we have to help and treat the final link in the chain—the parts we can see—and such treatment may be painful and unpleasant. It will be more so if the inner roots aren't found and exposed. War, for instance, is a tragic last resort that becomes necessary when humanity neglects the search for the roots of our problems.

So it is that common criminals must be prevented from continuing their law-breaking ways, and this must be done by imperfect law-enforcing establishments. If the solution could be found earlier, this drastic step could be avoided. We can all contribute to building a world in which vicious circles get broken before they result in wrongdoing; the cornerstone for this work is to examine our own reactions to authority that, left unchecked, can set an avalanche rolling.

#46 Authority

11

Bringing Ourselves to Order, Inside and Out

It's a miracle what an orderly place the universe is, every particle always in its right place. It runs like an immense wheel with infinitesimally meshing cogs interacting and complementing each other. We can barely conceive of the grandeur of this creation that couldn't exist without the principle of order underpinning it all; the mathematical precision of it escapes our vision.

In our fragmented view of things, we see things out of context, perceiving chaos and disorder instead of the greater order. What we see is in fact real—it's a consequence of our distortions. Chaos is even reflected in nature on our planet, with apparently destructive, cataclysmic events occurring as natural phenomena. Yet even in the colossal mess of a natural disaster, a larger order prevails.

Orderliness is directly connected with divine harmony and, like so many things, there is both an inner version and an outer version; there's also a divine version—order—and a corresponding distortion—disorder. Let's make some sense of how it all fits together.

In the grand scheme of things, inner order is what we experience when we are fully conscious and there is no more unconscious material left in our soul. Since that can be said of exactly zero human beings, order is something we're familiar with only in degrees. This is no different from how we experience other spiritual qualities like love, truth, wisdom, peace, bliss and reality.

So just when we get it all together and totally organized, we'll no longer be born as humans in this material plane of existence. Then we'll have tied up all our loose ends, putting everything into order. Conversely, any lack of awareness is an indication of disorder somewhere in our soul. When we're not aware, we're not in truth; things slip away into our unconscious and we become confused. As we grope in the dark, confusion interacts with disorder so that we struggle to patch together the fragments of half-truth at our disposal. We'll use anything to plaster up the holes and gaps of the chaos caused by our spotty awareness.

If we pay attention, most of us can see how this struggle goes on in our-selves. The disorderly mind will become frantic trying to impose a false order, but this only heightens our level of discomfort and disorderliness. It's like shoving garbage under our furniture so no one will see it, but the whole place reeks of the hidden waste.

In our psyches, waste is made up of false opinions and obsolete patterns of behavior; such things should be properly disposed of. If they stick around, all of our actions, decisions and perceptions will end up polluted by half-truths or out-and-out errors. The result: chaos and disappointment. Until we start making order of things through careful examination of our feelings and reactions, attitudes and beliefs, we'll continue to patch and repair until everything comes apart at the seams. False structures always fall apart. The most radical collapse happens when we die, which gives us the opportunity to start again with a clean slate.

Our day-to-day world is not a symbol of our inner life, it is an expres-sion of it. So anyone who hangs onto useless material, never cleaning out their closets or drawers, is of the belief they can create a functional order over a false order. We live in such an illusion at great expense.

So order and awareness are directly linked. Whenever we have disorder in our lives, there is something we are avoiding. Through our escape, we create the darkness of disorderliness. By avoiding something, we fail to create order in that area. So then here's another link: avoidance and lack of awareness. This is exactly what happens when we're not dealing with old emotional and mental baggage. It piles up and keeps new valid thoughts and feelings from finding a place to land. Self-awareness is what's needed if we hope to get things flowing smoothly in the proper channels.

On the material level, we clean our house. We might focus on our possessions or on our financial affairs or on our use of time. We may need to face and overcome a habit of procrastinating, which is a pattern of putting things off instead of dealing with them as they arise. Our object should always be to remove clutter.

The principle of orderliness works the same in our inner lives as in the outer. We must make a decision to devote time and effort to the smooth operation of our life. If we've accumulated a lot of garbage, we'll have to expend more effort to establish order. This is a great chance to form some new habits, learning to deal instantly with what was previously avoided. We focus our attention on whatever needs it most right now.

Then a new inner peace will set up shop. But peace will always elude us—no matter how much we pray and meditate and devote ourselves to spiritual or artistic endeavors—if we let inner and outer disorder clutter up our lives.

When we're busy avoiding something, we're escaping from what is. We don't know what's going on, inside or out, try as we might to hide our confusion and disorganization from ourselves. Every time we take the risk to face what we've evaded, it brings new light and order into our lives. We can literally feel an inner order and cleanliness that we previously lacked. But when we stay in not knowing, we remain mired in darkness and dwelling in discomfort.

When we live in disorder, we run from reality. We delude ourselves into believing that it won't impact our lives if we avoid dealing with what needs sorting. Silly rabbit. It's total illusion that our creativity is not impacted by sticking our head in the sand. Nothing we do or don't do, commit or omit, is without consequences. Not doing something creates conditions the same as doing something, and it all affects our level of comfort, peace and orderliness, or lack thereof.

Lack of awareness, avoidance and illusion are never going to add up to something good. They create disorder, which leads to more of the same—lack of awareness, avoidance and illusion. We can stay in this loop until the mind and the will wake up and decide to do something about it. They need to commit to sustaining order.

To be in awareness is to deal with the matter at hand, whatever it is, with laser-like focus. To be in reality is to be completely present with the effects of how we live our life. Awareness of reality creates the terms needed for order and harmony. Order, in turn, creates more ability to focus on our unfolding life and it allows more room for reality. This is a ring worth grabbing onto.

When we suspend ourselves in the illusion that any problem will go away by itself, we breed disorder. And that's what causes us to suffer. Sometimes, we'll lose ourselves in our disorder as a way to escape our suffering, but we're then up to our eyeballs in avoidance and simply not aware of our suffering. We then ascribe all our ills—our tensions and anxieties, pressures and discomfort, bad conscience and nagging discontent—to other causes. But this doesn't change the facts: we are the ones responsible for so much of our self-created disorder.

This applies as equally to the big stuff as to the little everyday occurrences. Neglecting even the tiniest thing can cause unrest in the soul, whether we're talking about a minor emotional skirmish or leaving things out of place in our home. The outer is always related to the inner in some way; it's good to pay attention to our habits and outer life while bearing this in mind. We can look around and get a good gauge on what's happening in our interior, noting how much disorder can divert our energy and scuttle up our inner landscape.

Orderliness isn't just a good idea, it's a spiritual principle. Its lack belies something about where we stand, inwardly. So someone who has their act pulled together is going to be an orderly person in their outer habits. They will be clean, not just in their body, but in their handling of daily life. Tasks won't pile up due to procrastination and following the path of least resistance. No, chores will be knocked off as they come up, even if that makes for a momentary difficulty, because the peace that follows makes it worthwhile.

The creation of order always asks for an investment of effort from us. A spiritually mature person gets this. We don't live in the illusion that comfort and peace of mind come for free. We've done the math and can see that the gains outweigh the investment, so we apply this formula to all areas of our lives. And we wouldn't want it any other way. We're willing to pay the price to live in a state of order. In return for our investment, we get to live in reality.

When we live in a disorderly way—in our personal affairs, our money matters, our approach to completing our tasks—a very insidious thing starts to happen. We become preoccupied with the disorder we have created. It does not occur to us that there could be another way, and we think that creating order would require energy that's beyond us. Nothing could be further from the truth.

Disorder is an energy sucker, wasting our energy by dissipating it and using it up. Order, by contrast, is a natural state, so the moment we summon energy for it—although there may be some activation energy required to make it up the first hill—energy will be released. Then more energy will become available. This is the energy that was previously being used to keep ourselves in the dark by avoiding reality and dimming our consciousness.

Making messes then comes from our unconscious negative intention—our will to stay stuck. This may be a whole new vantage point from which to view disorder. It exists for the sole purpose of resisting harmony and health, truth and wholeness. It creates tension and keeps us preoccupied, consuming valuable resources that could otherwise be dedicated to the task of finding God within ourselves.

Bold this: **disorder makes us anxious**, whether we're aware of this or not. Ignore what needs tending to and our life will slip away before our eyes, waiting to be lived another day. Fulfillment then gets put off for a future that never arrives.

If we get our work done in a timely way, we have control over our life; it's not hard to connect these dots. When we're in control, we don't avoid, procrastinate, let waste pile up or tell ourselves it doesn't matter. This is healthy self-control and these are necessary functions that the ego should be performing. To lack control is to create disharmony and imbalance. Then an opposite split-off condition of false control comes into play.

When we're over-controlling, we hang on too tight, holding ourselves together. But if we were holding ourselves together in the right way, using healthy control, we would be able to relinquish control when it is right to do so, and give in to involuntary processes such as our feelings. People who live with the right kind of ego control are able to surrender themselves in ways that people living in chaos cannot. Chaos makes it virtually impossible to let go of control because in doing so—without the self-discipline that comes with ego strength—we would drown in our own chaos.

This points up the need for self-discipline as an unavoidable prerequisite for finding spiritual fulfillment; it's what makes it safe to surrender to sexuality, deep feelings and the process of self-discovery. We are safe when we're standing in reality with a fully functioning ego that creates order and can therefore trust the process of letting go.

Order requires discipline. Always. Immature people tend to refuse any form of discipline, associating it with authority from a parent against whom a war is still being waged. This very behavior is part of the junk heap of waste material that needs our attention. The more we look for a parent-like authority figure to run our life, the more we rebel and the less we adopt attitudes that could lead to peace. We think that self-discipline is going to mean self-deprivation. On this, we are so very wrong.

Here's the real skinny on this: the more we refuse self-discipline, the more we deprive ourselves of all the rewards that come from a peaceful and comfortable existence. We keep ourselves from knowing the bliss and deep pleasure that are part and parcel of the involuntary life stream, and which can only flow through us when our ego stands on the firm ground of self-discipline.

Learning self-discipline then is the doorway through which we establish order. It all comes down to how we arrange our time, money, possessions, surroundings and personal appearance. We need to learn to take care of tasks as they come, orchestrating the details of our day so they will run smoothly.

We can devote some of our time and effort to creating new order, cleaning up old disorder and then sustaining it. If we run into a wall of resistance, we can sit with this in meditation, praying to know more of what it's about. We need to find the place inside us that says No—that doesn't want to give to life. What's *that* about?

If we can overcome our resistance and establish a new way of being in the world, we will notice a big difference. Burdens will drop away like icicles in the sun. We will have the clarity needed to resolve our problems and surrender to our deeper selves. When we put our control where it's needed, we can give up control where it's not.

So while it is true that outer disorder always reflects the state of the inner soul, which must be in illusion and out of order, outer order may not necessarily be a sign of having reached inner harmony. Often it reveals the exact opposite. Then orderliness is not a reflection of an inner clarity, but a compensation for inner disarray.

When we are compulsive in our orderliness, becoming anxious and afraid without our routines, that's a sign of inner disorderliness. If we feel burdened and obsessed about being orderly, needing it at the expense of feeling relaxed, expanded and free, the innermost being is sending up a flare to the outermost layers of our being: "Get yourself organized!" But the message gets garbled up in our resistance to communicating clearly inside ourselves. In all the clutter and debris, we're not deciphering our messages correctly.

Our resistance can be surprisingly strong. When we kick over to compulsive orderliness, we create as much trouble and hardship as if we were surrounding ourselves in filth. Sometimes this shows up to a minor degree, and for others, it can be very strong, manifesting for example as a compulsion to wash. The test for which condition prevails is to look carefully at the climate of one's life. If the atmosphere is easy and relaxed, and the orderliness creates more ease than strife, it's an expression of the divine principle of orderliness.

The first step in becoming aware of this connection between orderliness and our inner landscape is to tune into how much we are disturbed by disorder; feel the tension and anxiety it creates. Notice the resistance to self-discipline and consider what problems are difficult to make order out of. This new awareness may create motivation to begin tackling an issue from

the outside, rearranging outer aspects in a new way. This inner understanding may now make it possible to choose this option voluntarily, not as
an act of obedience. The latter wouldn't be very meaningful and more apt
to generate resentment and more resistance. It could also create a false
sense of guilt that serves no useful purpose whatsoever. We need to be
mindful of all these aspects along the way.

Interestingly, the part of us that resists is well aware that freeing ourselves of the burden of disorder will make our inner work much easier.
And that's exactly what the resistance wants to avoid. Think about it. The
disorganized person can't concentrate; same for the compulsively orderly
one. Being scattered makes it impossible to be focused. The mind wanders
and gets preoccupied with all that's left undone. It often wanders far away
from the disturbance. But if we follow its meandering, we'll start to realize
all the little things we don't want to tackle.

People who consider themselves creative or spiritual often feel that personal order isn't important. And yet, the great questions in life always rest
on the little ones. This is why it is said that when we sweep the corners, the
middle will sweep itself. Attend to the littlest attitudes and when they fall
into place, as creation does in even the tiniest detail, creative expression
will be less be hampered.

Don't make light of the power of this topic. And don't try to use outer
orderliness as a cover for inner work that must be done. As always, we
want to gently probe into our own behavior. Where do I create order that
leads to ease and relaxation? How do I resist doing so? In what ways do I
suffer from disorder? Can I feel the anxiety I cause myself? What are my
actions or inactions that contribute to this? How do I lose myself in the
wrong way, preventing me from losing myself in the right way?

Let's circle back to avoidance, which exists across the board. We try to
overlook seeing how we are dishonest, wanting to cheat life even if we
don't actually do it. We want to gloss over our destructiveness and avoid
seeing our negativity. These secret, invisible thoughts seem so harmless, we
delude ourselves into thinking we're not hurting anyone. We hope to avoid
all feelings that are inconvenient.

There is a price to pay for all of this: it's insanity. But if we are willing to confront ourselves, looking straight at the golden point in the center, truth and reality will suddenly appear. Arising right through the middle of the dreaded area will be the golden point of God, the unifying light of truth and purification. Because everything we avoid has, at its center, a golden point of light.

Go directly towards the golden center of any woe and it will dissolve. Go away from it, and suffering increases, along with confusion and darkness. We think some areas—such as our terror and our cruelty—are too terrible to contain such a point of light. Not so.

But if we avoid facing our terror and our evil, they live like phantoms inside us. These phantoms are creators of chaos and disaster. We need to turn around and face our inner demons, going into them, no matter how bad this feels at first. For each of us, this dark area is whatever we dread the most. But if we can summon the courage and honesty to turn toward the darkness, we'll come face-to-face with the golden point of light in our being, which is at its center.

This is worth repeating: the golden point of brilliant light is at the center of every horror, every death, every darkness. So every evil contains a golden point of light. This isn't a theory, it is a truth. And knowing this will help us to go through every tunnel of darkness, so we can arrive into the golden area of light.

#205 Order as a Universal Principle

PEARLS

12

The Right and Wrong Way
to Think Positively

We all have our doubts, and this is understandable. But many of us are hoping that when we come into contact with God and the Spirit World and the truth about it all, we'll be hit with some staggering proof that will wipe all our doubts away. Too bad it can't happen like that.

Doubt is the opposite of faith, with faith being basically inner certainty about everything we now doubt. And no inner experience can come by way of outer events. It just can't happen that way. What has to happen is that we prepare the inner conditions by removing our blocks and hurdles—in short, everything standing between us and true faith.

For the sake of argument, let's say we receive our hoped-for proof. But oops, we hadn't yet gotten around to clearing out all our obstacles. For a moment, we would be so impressed, saying 'Wow, this is wonderful, and strange, and amazing.' But once the glow wore off, the doubts would surface again. Then we'd say something like 'maybe that was just a coincidence.'

If the inner soil is not adequately prepared, the seed won't take. One level of reality can't replace the other, it can only be integrated into it. And that can only happen through slow and steady inner development. Experiencing absolute truth is like being with a live organism; it needs care and attention and nurturing and development. It can't come by way of a miraculous burning bush.

We understand this phenomenon as it relates to the growing human body. The growth happens so slowly, so step by step, we hardly notice it while it's going on. Then boom, we're at a new stage. The process is not an iota different for spiritual or emotional growth. Shortcuts and quick measures hope to eliminate the effort needed, but they never pan out with any lasting effect; they are the playthings of the forces of darkness. Slow and steady is the way to win this race, in accordance with divine law.

So no matter how astounding the experience, we can't get to spiritual enlightenment in one shot. Faith comes by methodically and persistently walking a path of soul purification, getting to know ourselves as we really are, understanding our conflicts and seeing the ways in which we sidestep spiritual laws. And if we're in conflict, divine laws are being stepped upon.

As we work, one step at a time, to free ourselves of our inner chains, our doubts will come less and less often. But they won't go away overnight. They'll just show up less often, until they disappear altogether. This, amigos, is the only way.

All divine processes work this way, by making progress little by little, leveraging personal effort to achieve anything substantial and permanent. We may not even be able to assess how our sense of faith blossoms as our growth process unfolds. This of course will be true for those just starting on a spiritual path of self-healing, but at various points along the way, we may be assailed by doubts, although often with lessening impact. Following is some simple advice for how to deal with these sporadic eruptions of doubt.

As we may know, there are two forces within the human soul. There is the Higher Self, or divine spark, which is the part of us that strives in the direction of perfection of the whole being. Our Higher Self desires integration of all our separated aspects; it knows the greater truth regarding anything we have doubts about, and it wants to bring this into our conscious awareness.

Then there's the other part, the Lower Self, which comprises all our faults and weaknesses, our ignorance and the attitudes that make us break divine law, whether we consciously intend to or not. This part fears the certainty of the Spirit World. For with knowledge comes responsibility, and the Lower Self wants no part of that. This part would prefer to stay ignorant—*if you don't mind*—and free from any obligation to overcome the ways of the Lower Self, which by the way is no small feat to accomplish.

So there's a yearning to know the truth of spiritual reality, which would mean eternal happiness and bliss, and which we doubt we can ever have, and which also—*did we mention already?*—is not easy to attain. So our Lower Self is working against our best interest, using its fear and its own reasons to make us doubt the Higher Self that desires to be in truth. It says, "it's for your own good, you know, to avoid disappointment."

So inside each of us, there is a battle going on between the Higher Self and the Lower Self. Wherever there is any disharmony, the two natures are at war. Whenever doubt reappears, it is Lower Self talking. When doubt disappears, Higher Self can be heard. That's when we know that God and his wonderful creation is the ultimate truth where it's all possible and unhappiness doesn't really exist.

It's when the Lower Self is stronger that we believe the voices in our ear telling us doubt and despair and hopelessness may be true after all. Here's the million-dollar question: which side is right? Who's telling the truth and who's talking trash?

What we need to do any time we're in a state of doubt is retire into silence. Then ask God: which is true? Then listen for an answer, which may or may not arrive immediately. In the coming days, just stay open to hearing an answer. It will always come.

Of course, what we may not sense in that moment is that the answer is already settled within. The mere fact that we feel depressed when we are in doubt, but we feel joyful when we are in truth, tells us a lot. Truth—even unpleasant truth—makes us happy. Yes, along a path of self-knowing, we are going to turn over some unflattering stones. But when our desire to be in truth trumps everything else, then even unpleasant truths will bring strength and renewed happiness.

Untruth, by contrast, has a knack for robbing us of peace, pleasant as an untruth might feel for a short bit. For deep down, our Higher Self knows the truth, and we feel that. Truth is not depressing. And in that is the answer to whatever question we haven't yet settled when we're sitting in doubt. So we can ask either our own Higher Self or God about the truth—in the end, they are one and the same.

Eventually, when we have overcome our inner hurdles and are mature enough to stay in a state of truth, those proofs we were hoping for will come from without—not once, but a hundred times over. These aren't proofs trying to convince us of the way of reality and to help us overcome our doubts; rather, these are proofs that will be more wonderful than anything we imagined, and they will arise naturally as a byproduct of the inner victory of navigating a path to God.

Short version: once we no longer need proof, we'll get it in spades. At that point, we won't need additional confirmation to be happy, as we will already be in truth. This means that whenever we doubt, we are not in truth. Pause a moment and take in this profound wisdom and divine law.

This brings up a subject of great dispute: positive thinking. As many believe, it is indeed essential for anyone who wants to mature spiritually. Unfortunately, it is often wrongly understood and therefore applied in the wrong way.

One of the fundamental building blocks of any spiritual path is developing clean and sound thoughts. After all, our thoughts have form and substance and are part of our reality. Unclean thoughts then build disharmonious creations that lead, eventually, to impacting our destiny. Our thoughts include not just our waking conscious thoughts, but also our emotional reactions and our unconscious thoughts. It's always so tempting for us to push uncomfortable thoughts out of our awareness, but we don't realize that those thoughts then have the power to do infinitely more harm than any conscious thought ever could—even our worst ones.

When a thought is conscious, we can deal with it. When it smolders in our unconscious, it's like a time bomb that builds highly destructive forms around itself. As a result, diligent students of positive thinking are encouraged to do the one thing that is the very worst for them: they push all negative thoughts out of their mind and into their unconscious, completely disregarding the discrepancy between what they actually think or feel and what they want to think or feel. All in an intention to not harbor negative thoughts.

So how do we parse the difference between our thoughts and our feelings? Thoughts can be controlled through the conscious direction of our will, similar to how we control our actions. But feelings cannot be directly controlled. For example, we may know it is sinful to hate, but that doesn't stop us from hating if hate is what's in us; we can't change this just because we want to. Similarly, we can't force ourselves to love a person, much as we might wish to. We can only affect a change in our feelings indirectly, by remote control, as it were. When we do our work of self-discovery, we naturally and automatically change our feelings. And don't forget, this takes time.

One way to go about this is to bring our unconscious thoughts into our consciousness. Positive thinking, however, attempts to work in the opposite way; it tries to convince us of out-of-sight, out-of-mind. Well-meant as this may be, it's a lie. And this is the real tragedy of the wrong kind of positive thinking.

Folks, it is imperative that we meet whatever exists in us squarely. Otherwise that part in us that doesn't like looking at unpleasant aspects is going to win. Then unconscious negativity ferments and works against us harder than our admitted negative thoughts.

So what's the right way to practice positive thinking? First, we need to watch our thoughts, observing them quietly and in a relaxed way. Pay attention to whatever emotions arise, noting they may or may not be parallel to our thoughts, and may or may not be what we want them to be.

We need to learn to spot our Lower Self in action, accepting the way it presently exists and knowing it's temporary—how temporary being entirely up to us. We can look away, but our Lower Self is a reality on this plane of existence and we can't turn a blind eye to any reality, on whatever plane it exists. Well, we *can*, but that doesn't make it any less real.

There's another way we misunderstand the principle of positive thinking. It springs from the fact that everybody wants to be happy. This is a natural wish of our Higher Self, which knows there is a price to be paid for it. The Lower Self, however, has the same wish to be happy, but not the same willingness to pay any price. The price is the effort one has to make to get to know all aspects of themselves, including all that's currently hidden. It involves overcoming our faults and learning spiritual laws—such as the law that there is always a price to pay for privilege.

The Lower Self, not surprisingly, wants to attain happiness through outer means and without paying the price of conquering itself. The basis for conquering our lower nature is being honest with ourselves, analyzing ourselves and coming to know ourselves. In its pride, the Lower Self wants to be perfect and not have to do the tiresome work needed to get there. The Higher Self knows that the only map to perfection is through the hard work of purifying the inner self. The Lower Self simply wants to have its cake and eat it too.

All our life difficulties are associated with our Lower Self and result from breaking spiritual laws in some way or another. As we mature, we become prepared to accept the workings of these laws as a way to honor God; we don't even try to get out of paying the price. Conversely, misapplied positive thinking wants to reach outer perfection quickly by learning thought control. This is a start, but it isn't enough.

The Lower Self latches onto this idea because it's such a good match for what it wants. But with true positive thinking, we accept the consequences for what we have done—whether in this life or perhaps in a previous life we no longer recall—saying, "I have to work out the effects of having broken spiritual law. Part of this means accepting the consequences I am facing right now."

One red flag to watch for is needing to practice—*very hard*—at positive thinking. The reason we sometimes try so hard is that our desire for happiness is emanating from our Lower Self, so we are inclined to quarrel with God. We might accept, in our minds, that God doesn't want us to be unhappy and have hardships, and that 'we create our own reality.' But emotionally, we don't really know this yet if we're still wanting something for nothing.

One price we must pay is to accept our difficulties, knowing they won't last forever. For God is love and wants only the best for us. But to be happy, we must accept the law of cause and effect, and we can't jump over effects through mere thought control. But nice try.

We can't be happy if we love our precious little selves in such a way that a little pain would be too unbearable. We must become detached enough from our ego to accept life's necessary pain, until eventually pain won't be needed for us to develop. Now don't think this means we should wallow in every little twinge, becoming resigned to hopelessness.

It just means we should realize that every pain we experience has been self-inflicted, and so we have to bear it, accept it, and most importantly, find its cause. That's how we eliminate it once and for all. How do we find the cause? By following a path of self-knowing (starting to recognize this refrain?). Find the fault responsible for the hardship and oust it at the root. During this gradual process, we can honor God by accepting spiritual laws. We need to shoulder our pain with courage and humility, not loving ourselves so much that we can't put up with a little pain. We can do this, knowing that experiencing a little discomfort is not the end of the world. That's the best way to practice positive thinking.

Fostering such an attitude will bring us the profound conviction that we have nothing to fear—God's world is a happy place and we have much we can look forward to. We'll automatically get recalibrated about time, sensing intuitively just how short the span of our little pain really was when viewed from a broader perspective. We make our difficulties into insurmountable mountains, when they are far more manageable if we're willing to meet them head-on.

Think of the Holy Scripture verse that says: "He who wants to win his life will lose it. He who is ready to give it up will win it." What do we think this means? It means that if we're holding on so tightly to our ego and our vanity, and are so afraid of a little pain we won't let go—we won't give up our life—we're gonna lose it. The "it" we'll lose is harmony and happiness, from within and from without.

But if we don't take ourselves too seriously, realizing the comforts of our ego are not oh-so-very important, and that a little pain or hurt vanity never killed anyone, we can give up our ego-selves and in return, come alive. We won't constantly be worried about what people think, or believing we can't show affection or true feelings without jeopardizing something. When we go with the laws of the universe, we'll find the love and respect we can't have when we're holding on too tight.

#13 Positive Thinking: The Right and the Wrong Kind

13

Uncloaking the Three Faces of Evil: Separation, Materialism and Confusion

For many people, discussing the topic of evil isn't easy. It wasn't always this way. For centuries, people could sense the invisible—the supernatural forces of lightness and of darkness, if you will. We saw their personification as spirit entities—as angels and as devils—and the influence they could have on humanity. So we fully recognized the power of evil.

At that time, what we lacked was the will to choose which would have the most influence over us personally. While of course we had free will—always have, always will—we were too immature mentally and emotionally to do much with it. As such, we didn't make wise choices. We let the Lower Self run the show, unable and unwilling to face and transcend it. In short, we were playthings of the dark forces.

Our lack of self-knowing led us to lacking self-responsibility. As a result, we felt like we were the victims of evil spirits. We feared them and became submissive to them. Some people even did this consciously and intentionally, openly worshipping Satan. For others, the choice to be influenced by Satan's world was kept hidden from conscious awareness, but of course this plays right into the hands of the Lower Self. We've then intentionally chosen to be ruled by the dark forces and no longer even realize it.

Roll forward a few centuries and eventually we became less and less connected to the invisible world. This disconnection, as we'll see shortly, is itself one of the hallmarks of the evil forces. But first, let's pause and notice for a moment how the manifestation of evil has embedded within it the medicine we need for overcoming evil, over the long haul at least. So while this disconnection from the supernatural had regrettable effects, at the same time, it snatched away our easy excuse that 'the devil made me do it.'

Now an arena has been created in which people need to look inside themselves if they want to fix the effects of evil. So this movement into isolation and separation from the world of angels and devils has helped us grow into self-responsibility. But now, as we ridicule what we think of as superstition—and it is superstitious to believe our fate is controlled by outside forces—we overlook the other half of the truth, which is that invisible forces do exist and do have their influence. In other words, we're stuck in a duality: either I'm responsible for myself, or the angels and devils are. Good news: by now humanity has matured enough to unite the two halves of this duality into one reality.

For people walking a path of self-discovery—whether through therapy, spiritual counseling or the like—the work tends to concentrate on waking up our own inner being, bringing all our inner obstacles into our awareness so we can transform them. This is important and necessary work. We need to get to know our Lower Self and how it operates if we want make another choice.

To the degree that we pray for help in purifying the distorted aspects of ourselves, and choose not to act out our Lower Self urges, we are protected against evil. To the degree we commit ourselves to aligning with our Higher Selves and following Christ's footsteps, dark spirits cannot approach us. But it's not enough to have goodwill and state our positive intentions on the surface, our decision must penetrate deeper into the hidden areas of our personality. This is the only way to become a shining light that repels dark spirits.

This means there are a few things we need to better understand, like for instance, how we are basically a big electromagnetic field that always follows the like-attracts-like rule. Bottom line: we need some information about the three basic principles of evil so we have a more complete and clear view of our lives and what we're up against.

The first and most obvious principle of evil is separation. This is readily associated with the devil whose greatest ambition has always been to destroy and inflict suffering. Satan, in fact—and by extension, our own Lower Self—is all about separation. This includes separation from God as well as from others and from ourselves. It shows up in our cruelty toward others, after which we delude ourselves that somehow we are not to blame or we are the victim rather than the perpetrator. We disconnect from where evil lives in us.

While separation is an aspect of all three principles of evil, it is important to identify the component of delusion in which we refuse to see that our brother and sister's pain as unavoidably also our pain. We ignore this basic truth, and on top of that, actually experience pleasure and excitement when we cause suffering and pain, and spread destruction. It's funny how much we do this, but not ha-ha funny.

Materialism is the second principle of evil. This applies of course to life on Earth, but it also applies to a whole host of hellish spheres we have had the misfortune of visiting prior to arriving here at the home planet. In those spheres, spirits live in a totally disconnected way, convinced that the dead state of dense matter they are in—way thicker and more condensed than what we're used to—is the only reality. Sound at all familiar?

Visionaries who sense what hell is like do not tap into the kind of suffering that exists in these hellish spheres. So here's an illustration. Imagine a world in which nature does not exist. Nothing is alive; nothing has flavor. Everything is so condensed, even a spirit's inner nature is inaccessible. Everywhere is nothing but deadness and complete alienation from anything with a pulse. All aspects of existence are mechanical.

With no birth and no death, this is an eternal life that is anything but heavenly—it's a gross distortion of eternity. This is hopelessness itself, as though change is impossible. Such hopelessness creates a suffering on par with the direct infliction of pain.

If we look at the history of life on Earth, we can see that up until fairly recently, the principle of separation manifested the most strongly. Over the past century or two, this principle of materialism has taken over. As superstitions have gone out the window, so have our connections to the more subtle aspects of reality. Our lifeline to the Spirit World has been broken.

The result? We have created an alienated reality in which we pride ourselves on our advanced state. In truth, we are living in a more advanced state due to our emphasis on matter and the technological progress we have made. But in this, we have become a reality onto ourselves. This has some upsides and some downsides.

The positive aspect of this is that it has brought people back to taking responsibility for themselves. It has caused us to search inside ourselves, to a greater degree, for what affects our fate. It's not coincidental that over this same period of time, the science of studying the human psyche has emerged, with psychology further facilitating our exploration and discovery. On the other hand, we have created a way of living here on Earth that is not completely different from that barren sphere of materialism described. It's like we've circled back to where we came from. Home sweet home.

Spiritually aware people have always known of these two principles. And since all principles and aspects of spiritual reality frequently manifest as entities, visionaries have throughout the ages recognized two different kinds of devils. Each ruled its own kingdom, with numerous lesser spirits serving it, since the hierarchy that exists in God's Spirit World of light also exists in the dark worlds, which are under the rulership of Lucifer.

The third principle of evil is not widely known. People may have vaguely sensed it more as a byproduct of evil. But hardly ever is it recognized as a powerful principle in itself, as effective as the other two in propagating evil. Like the first two, it has personification in the realm of darkness, with followers and its own hierarchy.

This is the principle of confusion, distortion and half-truths, which come in many shades and varieties. This is the evil of using truth where it doesn't belong, which subtly turns the truth into a lie. But such half-truths are hard to trace because they are presented under the guise of being divine truth, which makes them seem unassailable. The confusion that is created is not just a weapon used by evil people—it is a fundamental principle of evil.

These three principles of evil aren't hard to spot in our world. They are all around us, including inside us in our own Lower Self. They summarize, in fact, the whole mission and methodology of the Lower Self. In seeing this, we can start to become aware of when devilish forces are working away on us, trying to get us to destroy ourselves by inflicting pain on others.

They try to convince us of the illusion that we are separate and isolated—that there is no God and no life outside the boundaries of our current body. They use crazy-making confusion and false dualistic notions of 'it's either me or you,' along with half-truths and subtle distortions we cannot sort out. If we can start to see this in action, it will have a tremendous value for us. Because we can't fight an enemy we don't realize exists, and whose weapons we can't identify.

When we have some type of fault or wrong thinking in ourselves, we create a field of attraction that is like catnip for the powerful forces of evil. The only way to neutralize them and render them harmless is to align ourselves with God and remain true. We can use the light of Christ to do the healing work within ourselves, purifying areas that need attention so that we automatically, magnetically attract different forces.

Also know that just as different principles have prevailed over the course of history, with one stronger at one time and another at another time, so it is with each of us individually. Our own character will determine which one is in the lead at any point in time. But we can always be looking for all three, because they are all always lurking nearby. They all contribute to the aim of the dark forces, which is to alienate us and all of creation from God.

Here's an example of what it might look like when the three are in cahoots. Starting with confusion, we have a distorted take on reality, routinely looking away from the truth and instead making lies out of half a truth. This creates a certain numbness in us, because only when we are in full truth are we fully alive. From our numbness, which is created out of confusion and chaos, we inevitably inflict pain on others; lies must always lead to pain and suffering. Altogether, we have confusion that leads to numbness—a fundamental quality of materialism—and separation—the belief that my pain is not connected to someone else's. In this way, all three principles of evil coexist and reinforce each other.

Although many people dispute the idea that both good and evil could be personified, many others even dispute the notion that the principles of good and evil both exist. It's as if we think good and evil are just subjective perceptions. Here we are dealing with one of those half-truths mentioned.

So yes, we may experience good and evil in a limited, superficial way. Then later, when we explore an issue more deeply, we may discover that what we first thought was good is questionable, possibly even covering up evil. By the same token, what appeared on the surface to be bad may actually turn out to be a good thing.

So it's true, we should be cautious in assessing whether something is good or evil, using our discernment to examine issues in as much depth as possible. It's a grave mistake, though, to use this truth to jump to the conclusion that good and evil aren't real.

Denying the absolute nature of good and evil leads to hopelessness, skepticism, pessimism and a belief that the ultimate nature of reality is emptiness, nothingness—a void. For some time, it has been deemed fashionable and intelligent to postulate this type of nihilism. It expresses both the basic separation from the deeper spiritual reality, and dovetails nicely with an all-encompassing belief in materialism. Plus it contains the confusion and half-truth of denying the absolute existence of good and evil, which breeds more separation and causes more materialism. All in all, a powerful triple play of evil.

In this regard, we've come a long way. People are opening up to accepting God as a creative principle, even though we may hesitate to accept that evil principles also exist. We drag our feet more still though in accepting that all principles manifest on Earth as entities. We fear being called childish or primitive by those who are too smart to believe in such things.

But if the personification of principles and creative forces didn't exist, how could we? We're just a form of personification, personifying both good and bad by way of our Higher Self and our Lower Self. Isn't it more logical to think that beings exist who manifest more or less of each principle? And then shouldn't there be entities who manifest all goodness and total badness?

Regarding the latter, we might argue that all created beings are ultimately divine, so how can anyone be all bad? Well, in a much wider sense, this is true. But it may also be true that in their present human experience, their core is so covered over with evil that none of their goodness can get through. The long and the short of it is this: personification exists across the entire spectrum of good and evil, and to deny this is on the not-that-bright end of another scale.

Knowledge that we are surrounded and influenced by angels does not need to lead us to worshipping angels and overlooking Christ, who was God's human manifestation and who is the ultimate source of all the help we need. We also don't need to skip over making a connection with Jesus Christ, as that is what opens a direct line of communication between us and God. Being aware of the presence of spiritual guides and angels also shouldn't cause us to fear the devils, or dark angels, we attract from time to time.

As with any disease, the devils that come near us are cause, effect and medicine, all rolled into one. The fact that they are able to get so close and have an effect on us is due to our own limited and not-yet-purified parts. Our immature aspects draw devils near us who confuse us with lies so we can't separate truth from untruth. If we want to, though, we can use our confusion as a medicine. Because whenever it shows up, it tells us there is something in us that needs our attention.

Instead of denying that dark forces exist, we can overcome our fear and learn to distinguish their voices as different from our own. This is a very necessary step in our spiritual development. But if we deny they exist, we're not in a great position to counteract them. If we don't know that at times they are surrounding us, we become their tool. If we don't suspect that lies are being whispered into our thinking apparatus, we won't develop the ability to question and doubt the thoughts that filter through us.

We need to fine-tune our awareness of the connection between our Lower Self—best well-known for its ignorance and fear, destructive defenses and negative intentions, and lack of faith—and the voices of devilish entities. These two are partners in crime, forever wreaking havoc in our lives and the lives of those we touch. It's time to wake up to the facts, using our intelligence and fearlessness, so that we strengthen our connection with our Higher Self and its positive intention.

But if do this at the expense of paying attention to the insidious ways of the Lower Self, we'll become prey to evil influences. It's a bit of a grim reality that once we start doing the work of finding the truth in ourselves, we are a much more worthy target for the dark forces than someone who remains blind to their trickery and who has not dedicated themselves to knowing God. Not a bad reason to pray and ask Christ for his protection.

Now is the time when we need to learn as much as we can about what we're up against, to understand the weapons being used so we can combat this enemy force we've drawn to us. Remember, such engagement only happens to the degree we've not learned from periods of contact with them in the past, having failed not to turn inner disharmony into the medicine that it is.

So who exactly does Satan consider to be his opponent? Is it God, the source of all life and the creative principle in the universe? Is that whom Satan is directing his war efforts at? No, Satan, who is the ultimate personification of all three principles of evil, recognizes that God is the creator and he bends to God's will and God's laws. He can't not.

It was God's will, to be sure, that evil be allowed to have its sphere of influence and activities. For that's the only way that evil can be truly overcome in the soul of each and every fallen spirit—hint: that would be you and me. We're the entities who chose, through our own free thoughts and actions, to plunge ourselves into darkness. To ensure our safe return to God's kingdom, which would require us to ultimately overcome the evil inside us, God created very exacting laws and rules that prevent even Satan from acting outside of them. They also work to set limits corresponding to the will and choices of each entity.

So definite laws are in place then that govern the interaction between our Lower Self and evil spirits. Whenever we make an effort to question a thought—"Where is this coming from? Is this even true?"—the power instantly drains out of the dark angel whispering in our ear. It may be hard to feel this effect immediately due to our clogged up inner network, but the effect must come. This gives us some ammunition against being submerged by thoughts of untruth and confusion, getting drowned by them until we become so disconnected from the spark of life we suffer the pain of untruth and confusion. It is sad when this happens, and worse yet because it's so unnecessary.

OK, so if God isn't Satan's enemy, who is? It is God appearing in the personification of the Christ. Satanic spirits can't bear to be in the presence of this light of truth. So we can connect with the light of Christ and be protected from evil influences. But if we do this, we have a decision to make. Do we want it to connect us with the source of all life and use it to illuminate our way? Or would we prefer to unwittingly submerge ourselves in untrue thoughts and confusion because, in the moment, that seems so much easier? Heck, it might even seem exciting and fun. Of course, ultimately, if we chose the latter, we'll end up depressed that we have no faith that Christ will come and help us, bringing us the truth and clarification we desire.

So true fact: Satan's real rival is Jesus Christ, the one who came to Earth to open a way back for all of us caught in the morass of Satan's lair and weakened by his influences. This is precisely related to the idea of personification. When Christ walked on Earth, manifesting God here as a man who was both divine and human, he accomplished the most incredible feat anyone could imagine. He proved that it could be done: a person could remain true to God and to truth, and not succumb to the greatest temptations and influences ever unleashed by the forces of evil.

Through his unparalleled act of steadfastness, the man who was God made manifest and the God who clothed himself in human nature, opened wide the doors inside the souls of all created beings. Because he forged ahead, he made it possible that all souls submerged in darkness could gradually find their way back to the light. This is the way in which Jesus Christ saved every single entity who has ever been created, not to mention every speck of consciousness and energy that has ever and will ever manifest as a personality. Ever since Jesus came to Earth, this great light has been there for the asking, to help us build a tunnel back to the world of light.

Connecting with the light of Christ is like surrounding ourselves with an electric fence; when Lucifer's henchmen run into this light, they suffer physical pain. It contains all divine attributes, but this light of truth stings evil spirits. The light of love is wickedly oppressive to them, and the light of positive aggression—standing up for ourselves and for what's right—is terrifying to them. While the energy and consciousness of other divine qualities can be perceived indirectly by satanic forces, only the Christ consciousness can be directly visibly perceived by them.

We each may have an inking of how dark spirits recoil from the light of Christ. It has happened in the inexplicable reactions we've had in which we pull away from pleasure, from love or from fulfillment. We experience this to a much lesser degree than would a dark spirit. But there it is. We close up in reaction to receiving God's abundance.

At first, we're puzzled by this. But we can learn to observe this reaction in ourselves, just as we do any other destructive trait or irrational response. It makes so little sense that it can be discouraging when we see it, over and over again. Perhaps we meditate, visualizing ourselves opening to happiness, to love and to fulfillment. And still—wham. Shut tight.

Do we not see that hidden aspects of our Lower Self keep resisting exposure to the light? We can't stand it long enough to see what needs to be transformed. So prayer then is not enough, nor is meditating or visualizing. Using logic and having good intentions, also a bust. None of this will work as long as there remains a hidden agenda in our soul. In this area, whatever it is, we react the same way the satanic entities do who hide from the light of Christ. It's our hidden agenda that's the problem and that's what needs to be unearthed and brought to the light of truth. That's what is connecting us with the dark forces, making us their target.

So we can appreciate the demonic spirits' flight from Christ's light by observing our own similar reactions—the restlessness and anxiety that surfaces when great pleasure comes to us. And then we'll also comprehend what history has tried to convey: that the great adversary of Satan is Christ.

What exists on a small scale within the human soul, also exists on the greater scale. All our inner dramas are reflected in outer dramas, and the other way around. Every battle going on inside the human soul between the forces of dark and light—between the Lower Self and Higher Self—is also playing out on a universal level. Wars must be fought by all entities at all the different stages in our development.

So each of us will go through our personal battle within ourselves, and we will occasionally see our war waged with our surroundings. Last but not at all the least, we'll each become involved in issues on a grander scale that represent the universal battle between good and evil.

Our role in this battle—on whatever level it's happening—will depend on our current level of consciousness and the choices we have made for where we want to be. If we allow our off-kilter desires and immature emotional reactions to fog our vision—letting ourselves be carried along by the realm of darkness—we will become a target for all three principles of evil. Perhaps we will hide cruelty under the guise of 'just expressing our feelings;' we'll use gossip and the maligning of others as our tools of cruelty with the intention to hurt.

We might let our disconnection from the deeper reality blind us to seeing what's really going on. We'll get confused, using the truth to cover our lies and packaging lies as the truth. That's when we know that we let the forces of evil waltz in through the doorway of our Lower Self and set up camp. It's time to circle the wagons.

We've got to disentangle ourselves from this battle and not become tools for the prince of darkness. We need to marshal our goodwill to be in truth; see the hidden motives of our Lower Self to stay separate and disconnected; give up the line of least resistance and identify where we use the disorienting energy of negative pleasure to pull pain and destruction onto the heads of those we love.

It's so tempting to follow negative thoughts into the swamp. We get more and more fixated on the wrongs of another, blaming and accusing without regard for what is really true—the whole truth. *Including our part.* We prefer to believe the stories we tell and to continue to build cases against others.

The key to finding the way out is really quite simple. The first question to ask is always "What is the truth of this matter?" The second question: "Do I really want to know the truth?" Assuming we sincerely desire to be in truth—even if the only fraction of our being that currently desires this is the part willing to ask the question—these questions will dispel the clouds of darkness that tether us to the three principles of evil.

If we really want the truth, clarification will come. Even if the truth is that, in this moment, we don't really want to be in truth—we still want to blame and attack and see people in the worst light possible. We can't explore what this is about if we're busy pushing it away. So step one is always to be with what's here now. The truth will shimmer through slowly over time, if we are willing to admit that we have no intention to give the other the benefit of the doubt, to be curious, or to be in communication with them. This of course is what attracts those expert spirits of confusion and lies.

Being clear about what's true for us right now will dissolve the pain of guilt that we work so hard to keep under wraps. Our guilt causes us to project onto others what we're afraid to look at in ourselves. Clarity will also help dissolve the pain we inflict on others through the evil of our projections.

We like to kid ourselves that our negative thoughts and intentions don't really harm anyone else. But they inevitably are reflected in our actions and therefore affect others in insidious ways. Our thoughts simply can't remain isolated; they always lead to results and events in some way, shape or form. But our honest search for the answers to the questions about being in truth will bring much-needed clarity. We'll have new access to thoughts that were previously hidden from full view, but dishing out their dastardly effect nonetheless. This is the way to reestablish our connection with the source of eternal life.

The light carried in these teachings is always the light of Christ. Using this light, we can find our way to the truth in any issue, large or small, personal or universal. This is the way to find God who is the creator of eternal life, and who can only be found in the truth.

To find the truth, we will need to navigate the mazes of the dark areas of our own souls. We will run into the temptation to stay stuck and enjoy the thrill of our own negativity. We must deliberately work to overcome this temptation. The light of Christ is the overpowering love of all creation. We are blessed and protected when we choose this way.

#248 Three Principles of the Forces of Evil—Personification of Evil

14

Meditating to Connect Three Voices: The Ego, the Lower Self & the Higher Self

M editation comes in many shapes and sizes. We can sit and recite prayers, which is a form of religious meditation. We can also use meditation to improve our powers of concentration. In another kind of meditation, we might contemplate spiritual laws, or we may make our ego completely passive, letting go and following divine flux. All these have their own value.

There is yet another kind of meditation in which we use our available time and energy to confront the parts of ourselves that destroy happiness and wholeness. To be sure, we can never achieve the kind of wholeness we aspire to if we bypass this type of confrontation. We must give voice to the recalcitrant, destructive parts of ourselves that deny us the best life has to offer.

To get started, we need to understand the three fundamental layers of the personality that must be involved in the process of meditation for it to be truly effective. The three levels are: 1) the ego, with our ability to think and take action, 2) the destructive inner child, with its hidden ignorance and omnipotence, and immature demands and destructiveness, and 3) the Higher Self, with its superior wisdom, courage and love that allows for a more balanced and complete outlook on situations.

What we want to do in meditation, in order to be most effective, is leverage the ego to activate both the immature destructive aspects and the superior Higher Self. There must be an interaction between these three levels, which means the ego has some work to do.

The ego needs to have a single point of focus to get the unconscious inner child to show up and express itself. This isn't all that hard to do, but it's also not that easy. What makes it so difficult is that we're afraid of being seen as nowhere near as perfect as we want to be. We're not as evolved or as good or as rational as we like to pretend we are. We're selling the world an idealized version of ourselves that frankly doesn't exist, but our ego has bought its own story.

Our surface-level convictions about ourselves often clash loudly with the markedly different picture of what's hiding in the cracks and crevices of our unconscious. As a result, we secretly feel like frauds and are terrified of having this exposed. It's actually a sign of great progress when we can allow the belligerent little monster inside us to surface in our inner awareness. Being able to acknowledge this destructive part of ourselves in all its egotistical and irrational glory indicates a measure of self-acceptance and growth.

If we are not connected with our inner destructive parts, they can blindside us by manifesting undesirable creations that seem like they have nothing to do with us. If our meditation doesn't deal with this sort of blindness, it will be a lopsided endeavor.

It can be hard to accept that there is something in us that breaks away so decidedly from how we see ourselves and want to be. This part is an egotistical infant—an immature aspect of the Lower Self—and its antisocial desires need to be exposed in humbling detail. Meditation is a prime opportunity to encourage self-revelation, both in general and specifically in the way this unpleasant part reacts to daily situations.

So one direction to take in meditation is for the ego to reach down and say, "I want to see whatever is hiding in me. I want to see my negativity and destructiveness, and I am committed to bringing it all out into the open, even if it stings my pride. I want to be aware of how I refuse to see my part wherever I am stuck, and which makes me concentrate too much on the wrongs of others."

It is a tall order for the ego to expose all this on its own. It needs the help of the Higher Self, which is the other direction to turn during meditation. The Higher Self has access to powers far beyond those of the conscious ego, and they can be called upon to get the destructive little self to overcome its resistance and show itself.

The universal powers can also serve in helping to understand the destructive infant correctly, without exaggerating it. After all, we don't want to go from ignoring it to blowing it out of proportion. We can easily vacillate between self-deprecation and self-aggrandizement. We can also fall prey to thinking that ultimately we are that hot mess—that this is the sad reality of who we are. So it's important to not leave out asking for guidance from the Higher Self, without which we will easily lose perspective.

If we are an interested, patient listener, open to receiving the expressions of the destructive inner child, it will begin to reveal itself. Collect what surfaces and study it. We want to explore its origins in us. Why are we self-destructive? What are the underlying misconceptions that result in self-hate, spite, malice and our ruthless self-will? We'll find that once we uncover our hidden wrong conclusions about life, our guilt and self-hate will slip away.

We need to uncover the consequences to giving in to the short-lived satisfaction of being destructive. Our destructiveness will then weaken in proportion to our understanding of all the aspects regarding which cause led to what effect. If we gloss over this part, our work of self-discovery will be left half-done. We need to follow all the threads until we uncover exacting insight about our issues.

Meditation must go one step at a time, working in a three-fold manner through the entire problem of our unconscious negativity. We need to start with the observing ego committing itself to reaching in and exposing the negative childish side. The ego also needs to ask the Higher Self for help. Once the destructive parts open up, the ego again can ask for help from the greater self to guide the exploration of what it's all about and to see the heavy price paid to keep it going.

If we allow it, our Higher Self will help us overcome the temptation to give in, over and over, to destructive impulses. This giving in may not always show up in our actions, but often is present in our emotional attitudes. These are prevalent wherever we have conflicts, inclining us to concentrate on the woes of others or on circumstances outside our control. But instead, what would really help us is to explore how the cause for such problems is embedded in our own egocentric childish self.

For that, we need this kind of meditation, which takes time, patience and perseverance. We need to allow time for ingathering, being calmly determined to know the truth about a certain situation and its related causes. Then we need to quietly wait for an answer. In such a state of mind, we'll feel a peace come to us, even before we fully understand our part in our negative creation. Approaching life in a truthful way will also bring self-respect that was lacking as long as we held others responsible for our suffering.

If we are diligent in cultivating meditation for three voices, we'll discover a side of ourselves we have never known before. We'll realize how our Higher Self can communicate with us, helping expose our ignorant, destructive side, which needs insight and encouragement to change. It's only when we are willing to accept our Lower Self that our Higher Self will become a more real presence in us. Then we'll have a more clear sense that this is our real self, lessening our despair that we are bad or weak or inadequate.

Many people meditate but they neglect this two-sidedness and therefore miss out on the opportunity for transformation and integration. Their Higher Self may be activated, to the extent possible based on how free and open they are, but the unfree, closed off areas remain neglected. The work of opening and healing, unfortunately, doesn't happen by itself.

The ego has to want it and it has to fight for it. Otherwise the Higher Self can't get through to the blocked-off Lower Self areas. What's more, if we only make contact with one aspect—the Higher Self—this may lead to greater self-deception and make us even more prone to overlooking the neglected destructive side. Again, our development is at risk for becoming uneven.

Next comes the important step of reeducating the destructive inner child that is no longer completely hiding in the dark. We need to reorient the wrong beliefs, the stubborn resistance and the spiteful, murderous rage. But reeducation isn't possible until we're fully aware of all our hidden beliefs and attitudes. That's why it's critical we take such care with the first part of meditation: uncovering and exploring what's inside us.

Also note, this isn't a linear process. We don't get over the first phase before moving on to the second and then the third phase; the phases overlap. Further, there are no rules about when we should be exploring and understanding and when it's time for reeducation. They go hand in hand and we must continually feel into what's called for when.

Our habit is to overlook the stagnant parts of ourselves. So we might use the first meditational approach correctly, surfacing new aspects of the destructive child, only to neglect the second phase; perhaps we don't make all the connections between cause and effect, or we don't complete the reeducation process.

But if we track the whole meditation process through from beginning to end, we'll gain tremendous new strength for our whole being. Then several things begin to happen in our personality. First, our ego will become healthier. It will be stronger and more relaxed, with even more determination and single-pointed ability to concentrate.

Second, we'll have a better understanding of reality and more acceptance for ourselves. Unrealistic self-disgust and self-hate will dissolve. So too will our unreal claims of being special and perfect disappear, along with false spiritual pride, false self-humiliation and shame. All this accrues from the steady activation of our higher powers, making us feel less and less forlorn, lost, helpless and empty. All the marvelous possibilities of the universe reveal themselves to us when we tap into this wider world and it shows us the way to accept and transform our destructive infantile ways.

Gradually, as we work with meditation in this way, we will develop the strength to accept all our feelings. By accepting our petty, mean-spirited side—without thinking this is the totality of who we are—the beauty and wisdom of our Higher Self becomes more real. This is not a power that leads to arrogance and feeling special—those are Lower Self qualities. Rather, the result must be realistic, well-founded self-liking.

Where there is life, there must be constant movement, even if temporarily that movement is paralyzed. Consider that matter is paralyzed life-stuff; the frozen blocks in our body's energy system are also temporarily hardened life-stuff. This life-stuff, which is made up of both consciousness and energy—regardless of whether consciousness has been temporarily dimmed or energy momentarily frozen—can always be re-enlivened and set back into motion. But only consciousness can make this happen.

Meditation then is, above all, a process for re-enlivening frozen energy. The part of us that is already conscious and alert has an intention to reanimate blocked energy and dimmed consciousness so that movement and awareness are restored. The best way for this to occur is if the frozen and dimmed aspects can express themselves. For this to happen, we need to have a welcoming, receptive attitude, instead of a 'sky is falling, this is devastating and catastrophic' reaction.

Having a panicky attitude towards ourselves and what unfolds does more damage than the destructive child we are hoping to heal. We need to listen without hating ourselves for what we hear. Because this meditation will not be possible as long as we are denying and self-rejecting with a perfectionistic attitude. That won't allow us to unfold and explore, and it sure won't aid the reeducation process.

It takes a calm, relaxed ego to assert a gentle dominion over the violently destructive and stagnant matter of our psyche. Kindness and firmness will carry us much further than a bulldozer. We need to identify the destructive parts but not identify *with* them. Our best approach will be to observe in a detached way, without hurrying or judging. Accept what unfolds, knowing that its existence isn't final. Know too that we have the power within ourselves to change. It's when we're not aware of these aspects and the damage they do that we lack the motivation to change. So stay calm and remain detached.

Every day, in our meditation practice, we can start by asking ourselves, "What am I feeling right now about this or that? Where am I dissatisfied? What am I overlooking?" Right away, the ego can turn to the Higher Self for help in getting answers to these questions. Then we can continue an inner dialogue and ask further questions. If we're not willing to do even this much, we can confront *that*.

This is the only way for meditation to move us in the direction of problem resolution and greater growth and joy. Then trusting life won't seem like such a crazy idea. Self-love will awaken in a healthy sense that's not based on unrealistic expectations or wishful thinking. We'll discover that opposites can come into relationship with each other, and paradoxes can be reconciled.

To recap, the first stage of meditation is discovery, the second is exploration and the third is reeducation. Now let's discuss the fourth stage of meditation, which is desire. For people desire, and this is what expands our consciousness so we can create new and better life-stuff—and therefore life experience. Let's look more closely at the paradox of desire, since both desire and desirelessness are important spiritual attitudes. Only in the illusion of duality are they opposites, which leads to the confusion that one is right and one is wrong.

If we have no desire for more satisfaction or fulfillment in life, we have nothing to work with in re-molding life-stuff. We can't visualize a more complete state without having any desire for it. It's our ego that's in charge of fostering our concepts, and then calling on the Higher Self to bring them home.

Desire and desirelessness are not mutually exclusive, and if our ego has that impression, it can't grasp the right attitude for moving forward. In our desire lies our belief that new possibilities can unfold and greater self-expression can be enjoyed. But if we're all tense and tied up in knots about this, we form a block in our system. We're essentially saying 'I doubt if what I want can happen.' Under this may lie 'I don't really want it,' under which is a mistaken belief or an unrealistic fear or perhaps just an unwillingness to pay the price to have it.

All this underlying denial makes us tense about our desire. What we need to find and express is a kind of desirelessness regarding our desire: "I know I can and will have this or that I desire, even though I can't realize it right now. I have trust in the universe and in my own goodwill, and I can wait. It will strengthen me to cope with the short-term frustration of my desire."

There are a few common denominators that make meditation a rich and beautiful process with regard to healthy desire and desirelessness. First, we need the presence of trust and the absence of fear. If we are afraid of a little frustration, the tension inside us will prevent fulfillment of what we want. Over time, this will lead us to giving up all our desires. Then our desirelessness will be the wrong kind; we'll misunderstand and be in distortion.

In the final analysis, the real source of our tension is the infantile notion that we'll be annihilated if we don't get what we want. It's our inability to cope with not having that scares us. As a result, we're on a hamster wheel; our fear causes a cramp that turns into denial of our desire. This is what we can explore as we come into the fourth phase of meaningful meditation.

In this stage, we are expressing our desire, confidently sensing our ability to cope with both the fulfillment of it and the nonfulfillment. We trust in the loving nature of the universe to bring us what we long for. When we know that we will eventually realize the ultimate state of bliss, we can deal with the obstacles that arise along the way. Then desire will complement desirelessness, no longer at odds in an irreconcilable paradox.

Another seeming paradox is the ability for a healthy psyche to be both engaged and detached. Not surprising, we're going to need a two-fold approach to resolve this contradiction. We need to explore whether our detachment is actually indifference, caused by our fear of being involved and our unwillingness to endure any pain. If we won't take a risk because we're afraid to love, then our detachment is in distortion. On the flip side, if our involvement means we're super-tense, insisting in a childish way on having what we want when we want it, we've turned the idea of being engaged inside out.

A third and final example of how apparent opposites can be united into a comprehensive whole when they are not in distortion is regarding the inner attitudes of being active and being passive. If we're stuck in duality, we'll see these two as mutually exclusive. How can we be both active and passive at the same time, and in harmony? In fact, our meditation must do exactly this.

We are being active when we explore our inner levels of consciousness; we are being active when we struggle through overcoming our resistance; we are being active when we question ourselves about the until now hidden destructive aspects that show themselves; we are being active when we reeducate the ignorant nature of our young split off aspects; we are being active when our ego seeks out our Higher Self for guidance and help in healing; we are being active when we replace a limiting, incorrect idea about life with a new truthful concept.

Every time the ego reaches out to either the Higher Self or the destructive child, we are taking action. Then it's time to wait with patience, to passively allow the unfolding and expressing of both these levels. That's how we find the right blend of these two approaches—activity and passivity—in our meditation. Both movements must be present in our psyche for the universal powers of creativity to function.

Our goal is not to slay the destructive aspects of ourselves. No, these parts need instruction so they can be freed and allowed to grow up; then salvation can become a real thing. As we do this, our ego will, sure enough, move steadily closer to becoming unified with the greater Higher Self.

We only need to find where we are in distortion and where we are functioning well. Using this three-way interaction, we can create a harmonious blend of desire and desirelessness, of being involved and being detached, and of taking action and being passive. When this balance becomes our steady state, the destructive child will naturally grow up. It won't be killed off; it won't be exorcised like some kind of demon. The frozen areas will simply be re-enlivened and we will feel our re-energized life force waking up within us.

#182 The Process of Meditation (Meditation for Three Voices: Ego, Lower Self, Higher Self)

15

What's the Real Spiritual Meaning of Crisis?

C risis is nature's attempt to restore balance by causing a change that our ego has resisted. Our ego is that part of ourselves we have control over with our will—it thinks and it takes action. But if it obstructs change, the good and proper laws of the universe will come together and take over to effect change.

Crisis then is nothing more than a readjustment—a structural change—showing up in the form of upheaval and uncertainty, pain and difficulty, in order to achieve balance. Crisis could also just be the insecurity created when it's time to give up a familiar way and try something new. In whatever form it shows up, chaotic or coercive, crisis is always attempting to break down old structures that are based on negativity and wrong thinking. It shakes loose ingrained habits and breaks up frozen energy patterns so new growth can happen. Indeed, the tearing down process is painful, but without it, transformation is unthinkable.

Change is an inevitable fact of life; where there's life, there's never-ending change. Full stop. But when we live in fear and negativity, we resist change. In doing so, we resist life itself, which stops the flow of our life force and makes suffering close in on us more tightly; our resistance may affect our overall development or just show up in a particular instance. So then crisis comes along as a means for breaking up stagnant negativity—so we can let go of it. But the more painful the crisis is, the more our ego—that will-directed part of our consciousness—attempts to block the change.

Our inherent potential is truly infinite, and the intention behind human growth is to free our potential. Because wherever negative attitudes have settled in, realizing our potential becomes impossible. We can only be healthy and free in aspects of our lives where we don't resist change. When we're in harmony with the universe, we're constantly growing and feeling deeply satisfied with life. But where we have blocks, we cling to the status quo and hope nothing ever changes.

In the areas then where we don't resist change, our lives will be relatively crisis-free. Wherever we resist change, crisis is sure to follow. Our stagnant negativity creates a structure built on faults and errors and wrong conclusions about life; we're living in contradiction to the laws of truth and love and beauty. This structure has got to come down and crisis is the wrecking ball that will shake up the stuck, frozen areas in us that are always negative.

On any path to spiritual enlightenment, we're going to need to do some serious work if we want to free ourselves from our own negativity. What exactly are these negativities of which we speak? They include our misconceptions and wrong conclusions about life, our destructive emotions and the behavior patterns they give rise to, our destructive defenses and our pretending to be more perfect than we are. But none of these would be that hard to overcome if it weren't for self-perpetuating forces that compound in our psyche and keep picking up speed.

As we may know, all our thoughts and feelings are energy currents. And energy is a force that increases using its own momentum. So if our underlying beliefs and thoughts are in alignment with truth, they will be positive and the self-perpetuating momentum of their energy will increase ad infinitum. But if our concepts and feelings are based on error, they will be negative. This means the energy will compound, but it won't go on forever.

For example, when we have a faulty concept about life, this causes us to behave in a way that inevitably seems to prove that our assumptions were right. This entrenches our destructive, defensive behavior even more firmly in our soul substance. It's like this with our feelings too.

Our fears are always based on illusion, and we could easily overcome them if we were to challenge them and expose the fundamentally flawed premise on which they stand. Instead our fear makes us afraid of facing ourselves so we can transcend our errors. We become afraid of our fear, and then we hide our fear behind rage, or disguise it with depression. The fear compounds.

Or let's look at depression. If we don't courageously unearth what is causing the original feeling of depression, we'll become depressed about being depressed. Then we'll beat ourselves up, thinking we should be able to face our depression and not be depressed about it. But we got into this spot because we're not really willing to face it, therefore we're not able to, and that makes us more depressed. Next day.

Round one of a feeling—whether it's fear or depression or another difficult emotion—is the first crisis we didn't heed. We didn't work to understand its true meaning and in that, we evaded it. This launches us into all the subsequent rounds of being afraid of our fear or depressed about our depression. Caught up in such self-perpetuating vicious circles, we become more and more removed from the original feeling and from ourselves, which of course makes it even harder to find the original feeling. Finally we reach a breaking point. That's when the perpetual motion machine we've created has a breakdown.

Divine qualities like truth and love and beauty go on infinitely, but distortions and negativity never do. They cease abruptly when the pressure bursts. Enter, crisis. This is painful and we usually resist it with all our might. But what if things worked the other way, and negativity went on forever? Then hell could be eternal. OK, so then about that crisis.

The two places this negative self-perpetuating principle shows up most obviously is in the case of anger and frustration. We get angry at ourselves for being angry. In a similar way, frustration itself is easier to tolerate than our frustration about how frustrated we are. We get impatient with ourselves for our impatience, wishing we reacted differently but not able to do so because we haven't faced the root cause.

In all these instances, we are not recognizing the "crises"—anger, frustration, depression or impatience—for what they are, and that makes the wheel turn tighter until the inflamed boil bursts open. Then we have a real crisis.

The eruption of a crisis more clearly defines our options: figure out the meaning or continue to escape. We are given a means for exiting the ride, or we can keep going and be flung from it more painfully later. In the end, resistance really is futile.

Mystics speak of a "dark night of the soul," which is such a time of breaking down old structures. But we usually misunderstand this and look in the wrong direction. We need to search for inner truth, which means we must summon a tremendous amount of honesty to challenge our cherished, tightly held convictions. But cutting off the motor force that compounds our destructive cycles is a smart way to avoid pain and problems.

Just as a thunderstorm serves to clear the air when certain conditions in the atmosphere collide, crises are natural, balance-restoring events. But it is possible to grow without creating "dark nights" for ourselves. The price we need pay for this is self-honesty. We must cultivate the habit of inner looking whenever disharmony arises; we must be willing to abandon our pet attitudes and ideas.

Often, the biggest struggle in a crisis isn't about giving up an old structure, but about our straining and opposing new ways of operating and reacting. We can gauge the urgency of the need for change and the intensity of our opposition by how intense and painful the crisis is. Oddly, the event itself is not the litmus test, but rather our response to it.

It is possible that a traumatic outward event—the loss of a loved one, a war, illness, or loss of fortune and home—creates less inner pain and agitation than something relatively minor. This happens when, in the former case, we are able to adjust, accept and find a way to deal with the event. In the latter case, we, for some reason, may have greater resistance. Then we'll try to rationalize our disproportionate reaction, but this doesn't lead to lasting peace.

What does lead us to peace? First, it helps to accept the process of the crisis and not obstruct it; go with it instead of fighting it; then relief can come fairly soon. Second, we need to surface the wrong idea underpinning the negative experience. Every painful life event stands on error, and a critical aspect of our work is to articulate it. This is an incontrovertible fact, and yet how often does this manage to slip our mind when we meet an unhappy situation?

So far, we've been focusing on the negative aspects of self-perpetuation. What about the positive side? With love, for example, the more we love, the more we can extend genuine feelings of love and our giving won't impoverish anyone. On the contrary, we'll increasingly find new and deeper ways to give, and more will come to us and others from it. Experiencing and expressing love builds momentum.

It's the same with any constructive, joyous, fulfilling attitude or feeling—the more we have, the more we must generate. Steady expansion and self-expression ripples outward in a never-ending process once we tap into the innate wisdom, beauty and joy of our Higher Self. The initial effort to establish contact and actualize these powers takes some effort on the part of our ego. But once we get the ball rolling, the process is effortless. The more wonder we bring forth, the more there will be.

It bears repeating that our potential to experience creativity and pleasure, beauty and joy, and wisdom and love, is infinite. But how deeply do we *know* this reality? How much do we believe in our own resources to solve all our problems? How much do we trust in the possibility of all we have not yet manifested? How much do we believe that we can create new vistas? How much do we realize we can couple excitement with peace, and serenity with adventure, making life a string of beautiful events even if initial difficulties must still be overcome? How much do we believe in any of this, people?

Let's connect some dots: to the extent we pay lip-service to these beliefs, we will still feel depressed, hopeless, fearful or anxious; we'll remain tied up in the tight knots of conflict. Because we don't yet believe in our own infinitely expanding potential. That's because there's something inside that we're desperately hanging onto. And we don't want to bring that out into the light because we don't want to give it up or change it.

Perhaps we give in to the dangerous temptation to project our experience onto others, blaming them for our misery. Or worse we might project them onto ourselves in a self-devastating way. We avoid our issues with attitudes like 'I'm so bad, I'm nothing,' which is always dishonest. We need to expose this kind of dishonesty so that our crisis, whether large or small, can be meaningful.

This applies to every single person in the world. For whom among us hasn't had to put up with more than a few "dark nights"? But if we learn to explore even the smallest shadow for its deeper meaning, no painful eruption of crises will be needed. There will be no rotten structures that need to be destroyed. In this, the stark reality of life will be revealed to us: we have the golden opportunity to live in ever-expanding joy. Then the sun will rise and our dark night will prove to be the educator—the therapist—that life can be, once we try to understand it.

How often do we find ourselves faced with negativity from someone else, but we're not sure how to handle it? We feel anxious, uncertain and not clear about how to interact with them. We may not directly feel their hostility, but are confused by their indirectness or their evasion. We feel guilty about how we respond to them, which makes us even less able to handle the situation.

This frequently happens when we are blind to our resistance to change. We project all our unattended-to baggage onto the other, making it impossible to be aware of what is actually going on in them. Then we don't know how to handle things. But when we start to handle our own selves, growing in our capacity to honestly look at what disturbs us and becoming willing to change, we'll "magically"—as if it had nothing to do with us—receive a gift: we will see others negativity in a way that frees us, while providing a way to confront them that is effective.

Our catch-22 is that we resist changing and fear growing because we sense an inevitable breakdown is steadily drawing nearer. Yet we resist doing what we can to avoid the crisis. This is the story of human life; this is where we're caught. As such, we must keep repeating the lesson until we learn that our fear of change is an error. If we can expose this illusion, our life will open up almost at once.

Change, however, cannot be accomplished by the ego alone. The willing, conscious part of ourselves is incapable of doing it alone. A significant portion of our resistance and difficulty with changing comes from having forgotten that this is not a job for the ego. We need divine help.

Our forgetfulness sends us careening from one extreme to the next. On one hand, we think we must accomplish inner transformation by ourselves. But we know we don't have what it takes to do this on our own, so we give up. We feel it's hopeless to change and so we don't really try; we don't even clearly express our desire to do so.

From the perspective of the ego-self alone, we're right to think we don't have the capacity to change. We resist as a way to avoid the frustration of wanting something we don't have the tools to create. Disappointment is realistic for the ego. That, deep down, is what our ego is contemplating. Meanwhile, we're professing a belief in a God or higher power who is supposed to do all this for us. We're totally passive, waiting for it.

In short, we're not trying where we should be. We flip from false hope to false resignation, which are two sides of the coin of absolute passivity. The pushy ego that attempts to outstrip its limited capacity is going to land back in the lap of falsely waiting or falsely giving up hope—either alternately or simultaneously—wearing itself out in the process and rendering itself passive.

To make real positive change, we have to want it, and we have to be willing to be in truth. We need to pray to the divine living deep in our soul, then wait for the change to happen. We must wait with patience, confidence and trust; this is quintessential for change to occur.

Our prayer expresses this sentiment: "I want to change, but I can't do it with my ego alone. God will do it through me. I am a willing and receptive channel for this to happen." If we're not willing to say such a prayer, then we're not really willing to change. We still doubt the reality of the higher forces inside ourselves.

Don't fret—all is not lost. We can acquire this confident, patient waiting and trust that help will come by being utterly willing to be in truth. This isn't the childish attitude of wanting God to do it for us. Nope, this time we're taking action and facing ourselves; we're accepting adult self-responsibility; we're wanting truth and change; and we're willing to expose our hidden shame. We also know the limitations of our ego, so we can relax.

This is how we let God into our soul from deep within; we open up for it to happen. Change can become a living reality for anyone and everyone who adopts such an approach. Our lack of faith and trust that the divine can be activated from within us is only because we haven't given ourselves the chance to experience the stark truth of this reality. And how can we possibly trust something we've never experienced?

If we are willing to commit ourselves, we will let go of the old shore we're used to clinging to and float in momentary uncertainty. But this won't bother us. We'll feel safer than we did when we were hanging onto the shores of our illusions, the false structures that must collapse. Soon we will realize there is nothing to fear.

We must call up all the courage we can muster, only to realize this is the most secure way to live—letting go and expanding into life. We'll see the truth: living this way is natural and takes no courage at all.

#183 The Spiritual Meaning of Crisis

16

Mastering the Art of
Stepping into Leadership

These teachings are constantly urging us to open up, to let go of our defenses and the brittle hard shell we think we need for protection. We fear that if we are in an open, vulnerable state, painful negative experiences will be able to pierce us from the outside.

But we also must realize that lovely qualities like beauty and love, wisdom and truth, can be taken in from the outside. And that as long as we keep our defenses firmly in place, we block these from getting in too. So what happens is that people actually give us their best and life tries to give us what we long for, but we can't let it in.

Opening up works in two different directions, not just toward the outside. If we are willing to open up, we make it possible to allow the deepest levels within to unfold and come out to play. Since those negative, protective layers are obscuring the perfection at our core, they are going to surface first. But beyond them lies the pearl—the most creative and positive reality of who we really are. If we commit ourselves to being completely open and to remaining undefended, it will emerge.

We are under the mistaken impression that if we are open, we won't be able to protect ourselves from being abused. We couldn't be more wrong. Only by having a free-functioning Higher Self, being free from selfishness and being true to our innate integrity and sense of decency, following divine spiritual laws of justice, truth, wisdom and love—only then are we strong enough to safely assert ourselves and confront others. Only then will we be free from guilt and the associated anxiety and insecurity, not to mention unfounded fear and confusion—the real culprits that rob us of our ability to defend ourselves against abuse.

We need to think of opening up—of losing our defensive strategies—not as an act that is directed outwardly, but more importantly as an act of receptivity toward our inner self. Doing so requires courage and faith in our truest, deepest perfection, so we can allow the outermost layers of our Lower Self to show themselves. This is the only way to identify and purify them.

If we are far enough along on our path of personal development to open ourselves up to transforming our Lower Self, we are also capable of experiencing tremendous joy and fulfillment—along with genuine leadership. What does leadership entail, in its truest sense? And what should be our attitude toward stepping into leadership, in whatever field or direction it presents itself?

When it comes to leadership, we have many conflicting attitudes. First of all, we envy leadership when we encounter it in others. We often feel competitive, but try to conceal this from ourselves, which makes us resentful. So we set about building cases against those in leadership, justifying our judgments and rationalizing our unjustifiable thoughts and feelings. We reactivate our dormant reactions towards anyone in authority, dragging obsolete problems out of hiding and making an enemy of anyone who is a leader in the truest sense of the word. We think they are out to punish and deprive us.

In our envy of the leaders, we want to become the leader. But this undeveloped, childish part—which overshadows the parts that are more developed—doesn't want to accept any of the responsibilities that go along with being a leader. This sets up a painful dichotomy. In one respect, we battle against leadership in others, resenting and envying them; in another respect, we want to be the leader ourselves, but we don't want to fulfill the basic requirements.

We then resent those who are the true leaders for 'taking it from me,' or for 'not giving me the goodies' of being a leader. What we don't do is move toward adopting the commitment or the attitudes that are needed for leadership. Seen from this vantage point, our position toward leadership seems a bit absurd. Yet this is not uncommon, and once we identify it in ourselves, we won't find it so hard to see it when it arises again in ourselves or in someone else.

We have another common conflict with leadership: we want a leader who will benefit us personally. We want someone strong and powerful who is kindly disposed to us and exclusively concerned about the desires of our Lower Self—so we can indulge in our destructiveness and not have to face any consequences. This greater leader—really more like a biased personal god—is supposed to alter the laws of life for us, as if by magic. We should receive every privilege and not be required to love or give or take responsibility or be fair or have integrity. Honestly, there is no exaggeration here; this would be our perfect leader who will meet our irrational demand, which we are busily trying to justify.

But there is no justification for the cases we build against leaders. As long as we refuse to fulfill the natural requirements for leadership ourselves—in whatever way we are called to do so—we have no right to resent or envy leadership in others. Yet we do. The word that describes this phenomenon is "transference"—we react to this super-power the way we react to our parents.

The equation is simple: if we don't assume leadership over our own life, we will need to find a leader who will run our life for us. For no one can live without leadership; we become a boat without a rudder. So naturally, if we don't want to chart our own course, someone else will have to do it, at least to some degree.

On a neurotic level, we are going to ask for leadership to govern our life in a way that cannot be given to us. We'll want them to lead when it's convenient for us, but we will resent them for doing it. We will want all the freedom and privileges given to us, but won't step up to self-leadership. We're torn in two by our own hidden conflict.

We need to take a good, hard look at ourselves: are we still so undeveloped that we need someone else to lead us? Or are we ready to step into leadership in our own right? We begin by looking close to home, at our own life, and then see how we are ready to take responsibility for being a citizen of this world. Our leadership may take a different form for each of us, but it starts with the almost unnoticeable attitude we have towards our immediate environment. We start by taking simple steps of added responsibility.

It doesn't hurt us to uncover and examine destructive attitudes if we are in the process of dealing with them. While we're learning and battling and discovering more on ever-deeper levels, we're right where we want to be. But it is very damaging for us to stay stuck in attitudes we have outgrown. Too often, we fail to move on from our Lower Self habits, continuing to blame others for our ungiving ways, for our competitiveness or jealousy or lack of concern.

But the law of growth requires we now make different choices whenever the old negative reaction occurs. When we have greater self-honesty and self-awareness, the remaining areas in us that are still stagnant and stuck will have a heavier impact. This is important to realize.

Let's look at how this relates to leadership. We must look at how we resent those in a position of leadership, as though they are depriving us or imposing something unfair on us. We need to avoid acting as though we're being stopped from realizing our own capacity to be a true leader.

In truth, above all else, a true leader is someone who wants to give unselfishly. So if we are the leader and we are grudging about giving, doing it only because we feel it is demanded of us, well, this can't really be called giving. In the end, if we won't give in an unselfish way, we can't assert our leadership.

It is a spiritual law that there is always a price to pay for having what we want. So in some ways, it could be said that true giving is demanded of a leader—this is the price we must pay if want to have the privileges of leadership, of which there are many. Yet we feel the price is too high; we are outraged and we rebel, managing to justify our bad behavior.

If we do give, our way of going about it leaves much to be desired. We give begrudgingly or with ulterior motives; we have second thoughts or we calculate hidden inner bargains while leaving little back doors open. This is not really giving, which is why it leaves us and others feeling empty. We may then stoop to such low attitudes as, "See, I gave, and what did it get me?" revealing that our giving was not genuine, and at the same time, cleverly shoring up our resistance to giving.

Giving is more than a simple act; it is also the thought and the intention behind the act. The basic thought behind true giving is, "I want to give to enrich the world, not to aggrandize my ego. Make me an instrument so that divinity can flow through me, without my having any motive other than to give." This thought, ironically, will bring us many advantages. It will give us self-esteem and allow us to feel that we deserve to partake of the abundance we so often grope for desperately. When such a fault-free giving atmosphere permeates our inner climate, then we will no longer feel jealous; no one else's giving will have any bearing on our own. All this we will experience firsthand.

If, on the other hand, we fake our giving, life's abundance—including other people's giving—will not be able to reach us. Simultaneously, we'll envy those who are appreciated for their true giving—for the material and emotional abundance they receive. This, in itself, can be a good measure of where we stand regarding true giving, which is an act of love.

If we don't love and we don't want to learn to love, we can't expect that our deepest longing for love is going to be fulfilled. So while we're busy praying for love, we may be totally blind to all the areas where we could be giving but are demonstrating the opposite behavior. Leadership, in this sense, is built on a love of true giving and the true giving of love. When this is our basic attitude, nothing can go wrong. We'll be able to find a perfect balance related to all our conflicts, and resolve the difficult-seeming decisions we must make on this dualistic plane.

Another quality that is a prerequisite for leadership is the ability to be impartial. Often, we refuse to be objective about our personal stake in an issue, building justifications around our tainted desires. A key to reaching objective detachment is to develop the ability to see where we are partial. We need to admit it and extract ourselves from arguing about these cases, to fess up to how we bend reality to meet our off-center desires. For this, we will need some rigorous self-honesty.

We need to see how we have a stake in our assumptions that we're not open to seeing differently, all the while proclaiming how objective we are. But this is impossible. For when we're blinded by our own self-interest and self-righteousness, by our unfounded resentments and irrational demands, by our illusory fears and unnecessary guilt, by our covetous and jealous reactions, our take on things can't be objective.

It's an indication of greatness for us to know that we are filled with disturbing and turbulent feelings, rife with inner conflict, and therefore can't form a partial opinion. When we can truly know this about ourselves, we take a giant leap toward freedom and having the capacity to be a reliable leader people can trust. And that's the only way we will be able to validly and objectively assess others.

To be a good leader, we must have this greatness. If we don't and we have gained a position of leadership, we will be toppled by this. If we can't admit where we are partial but instead claim we are free from such inner hurdles, then proclaiming our "unbiased opinions" will make us very vulnerable. We will end up needing to continually guard and defend our unrightful role of leadership.

Our objective here is to know when and where we are not able to be objective. Having the honesty to admit that we're not impartial and don't wish to be will bring us self-trust and security. It takes great strength and maturity to voluntarily disqualify ourselves when we know that our view of reality is colored. Such greatness will increase our capacity to accurately perceive reality, knowing it as a state that doesn't need to be feared. And we'll be willing to stay true to it, even if that exposes us to criticism.

This brings us to another quality of leadership: the willingness to risk exposing ourselves and being open to criticism. If we close ourselves up in fear, while at the same time grabbing for the brass ring of leadership because we like the perks of power and prestige, we defeat the purpose. This creates a painful inner conflict that leads to frustration. True leadership can't survive under these kinds of circumstances. Of course, we won't realize this while we're busy blaming the outside world and the people who have already rightfully reached some level of leadership.

To be a leader means to constantly take a risk. We need a firm footing so we can tolerate the discomfort of being criticized and misunderstood, whether rightly or wrongly. But if we don't want to take any risk, and instead are filled up with jealousies, resentments and rebellions against other true leaders, how can we stand up for ourselves?

As leaders, things won't always go our way. So it will also be critically important that we develop our ability to withstand frustration. More than this, if we want to become whole and truly unified people, we will need to reconcile the apparent dichotomy of these two opposites: frustration and fulfillment. This can't happen if we are fighting against one half of this duality and grabbing for the other.

The hallmark of any duality is having a strong 'I must have it' towards what we desire, and an equally strong 'I must not have it' towards what we don't. This is a painful spot to be in. We attempt to let off some of the tension by pressuring life into giving us fulfillment and eliminating frustration. As a result, we never learn to transcend frustration so that it no longer occurs. Instead, our futile efforts to get rid of frustration can only make us more frustrated, pointing up that we have more to learn about frustration. Being caught in duality is such a drag.

So what would be a more fruitful way to approach frustration that might actually help us transcend it? First, let's be clear that we're not talking about a false transcendence where we disconnect from our feelings so we no longer feel just how tense and anxious we are about landing our desires. No, we're talking about genuine transcendence in which we're fully alive and feeling all our feelings, flowing in harmony with the stream of life. Like, not at all frustrated.

Here are the steps we should take to climb the ladder out of frustration. The first step is to foster an attitude that says, "Even if what I experience is painful or undesirable, I am going to trust it. I will trust that I can take it, relax into it and learn from it. I'll handle it by making the best of it. I will learn whatever this particular frustration can teach me, and won't act like this is the end of the world. Perhaps it's not even really a catastrophe, as something good could come of it."

Just resonating with such a statement will greatly reduce our level of anxiety and greatly increase our feeling of security. We're anxious because we think we depend on something that can't be. We think we are going to need to manipulate reality to get our immature need for instant gratification met. We think everything has to go according to our limited vision of things, which is not connected to the grand time-sequence of cause and effect.

So in this first step, we are making space to relax our reactions of utter disgust and outrage that frustration exists. We're afraid of being frustrated and are angry about it, but we don't think to challenge this reaction and consider that maybe it's not the only possibility. We need to make room for a new strength and a new wisdom to unfold that will help us deal with whatever doesn't bend to our will. Such an open attitude will bring us far more self-confidence and self-reliance than always having our way ever could.

Clearing the first step on the ladder of overcoming frustration brings us to the next step, which is a much more beautiful one. This is a renewed and deliberate search for the meaning of a specific frustration. What does it have to teach us? Never lose sight of this truth: every frustration contains a valuable lesson that can liberate us and bring us joy. Too often, we are not at all willing to believe that this is true.

We get so bent on battling every possible flare-up of frustration that the lesson gets lost on us. Whenever this happens, we've missed a golden opportunity on our spiritual path of awakening. And that means the frustration must, naturally, pass our way again. It must keep coming, no matter how hard we resist it. The more we battle, the more rigid we become, the worse the frustration seems, the more intense our feeling of frustration, until we're overwhelmed by it.

There's a chance that in the crisis of being overwhelmed, we'll discover how we have created the illusion that frustration is the enemy. This has the capacity to loosen us up so we feel less tension against the frustration and towards life. Frustration, folks, is our friend. We can make peace with it by intelligently exploring its meaning and courageously letting it be our teacher—as well as our therapist.

The next rung on this ladder is the discovery of the meaning of the frustration. If we knock, the door will be opened; all who search must find. And no doubt, we will always be astounded by what we discover. Once we

146

realize how necessary the lesson was for us, how important the answers we gained from our new wisdom and liberation, we will have an already-altered outlook about frustration. Then, when another lesson comes along, we won't be nearly so afraid of it. We'll have more confidence that it holds a measure of meaningfulness for us, and this will make us less resistant to repeating the steps.

The new trust we gain about life will help us open to the benevolent and magnificent consciousness that is behind all things, including frustration. Obviously, this will go a long way in reconciling the apparent mutual exclusivity between frustration and fulfillment.

The last rung on the ladder will walk us into a deeper and more radiant world as the point of frustration narrows. Having learned the lesson it had to teach, we can let ourselves fully experience that point of frustration. Sitting relaxed in meditation, we can flow with it, go with it, accept it and embrace it. Deep in the one-pointedness of our now-acceptance—which was previously rejection—we will discover the divinity of a particle of frustration. And it will no longer be frustration. It will miraculously bring us the highest fulfillment imaginable. We will gain so much more fulfillment than we craved when we were running away from the frustration.

In this, we will experience the way in which God exists in every particle of creation: in every fragment of time, in every fraction of measurement, in every slice of experience. The great divine reality of joyful truth and meaningfulness lives in everything that is, ever was, and ever shall be. We may have heard these words before; through these steps, we can know them to be true.

#237 Leadership—The Art of Transcending Frustration

17

Discovering the Key to Letting Go & Letting God

If we will listen with our inner ears, see with our inner eyes, feel with our innermost being, and give our doubting minds a rest, we can each find exactly what we need for our self-development. With this in mind, let's go deeply inside the phrase 'let go and let God,' a much-loved phrase in which there's more than meets the eye.

"Letting go" means to let go of the limited ego, with its narrow understanding, its preconceived ideas and its demanding self-will. It means letting go of our suspicions and misconceptions, our fears and lack of trust. Moreover, it means letting go of the tightly held attitude that says, in so many words, "The only way I can be happy is if so-and-so does such-and-such. Life must go exactly according to my plan."

It often seems we're being asked to let go of some precious thing that, in itself, is a legitimate desire we should be able to have. So does letting go of the little ego's self-will doom us to settling for less than our heart's desire? Must we be unhappy and unfulfilled forever? Is it wrong to strive for fulfillment? Or are we supposed to let go of that too?

The ultimate aim of "letting God" is to activate God from our heart center, from the innermost place of our being where God speaks to us if we're willing to listen. But before this highest, most secure and blissful state can be reached, we may need to do some housecleaning, removing obstacles and clearing up dualistic confusions.

It often happens that we are able to comprehend a great spiritual concept in general terms, but we can't see how it applies to our daily life. We think our everyday reactions to our puny little problems are too mundane to be connected with the greater issues of life. Yet it is only by making the connections in our so-called insignificant areas that we can uncover the key to our conflicts and the confusions—those things which make it impossible to apply great spiritual truths to our lives.

Like all things, any great truth can be distorted and handled in the wrong way. Take, for instance, the truth that we live in a loving, giving and abundant universe and we are not required to suffer. We might believe this but then go about overusing our will—called using a forcing current—in an attempt to get what we want.

To say we must let go of our forcing current seems to imply we have to resign ourselves to emptiness, pain and suffering—that our longing will never be fulfilled. In an effort to avoid this, we hold on tight, squeezing out the influx of energy that ushers in the world of light and love and truth and abundance—all the good stuff.

This divine influx can only flow when it is let loose, allowed to follow its own harmonious rhythm. So there can't be any hard knots of energy prohibiting the divine flow, such as our self-will creates through its distrusting, insisting, anxious forcing current. These qualities belie an imbalance of trust. What's being trusted is the little, limited ego, while the greater divine self—the Higher Self—is being denied and pushed away. This doesn't mean we should be denying the ego, but it needs to expand its wisdom and creativity, allowing the divine influx to flow freely.

All of our various attitudes create energy systems. A tight holding-on attitude results in a closed energy system, which is not hard to observe with our regular eyes. We see it in the way the creative spark is squelched wherever a few power-driven people impose their will over others. Such domination stems from fear and creates more fear. It also creates a closed system that generates resistance, although out of their own fear and weakness, people may temporarily submit to such tyranny.

But eventually the time must come when each and every fearful person will stand up and throw off the chains. If we look back through history, we can see that this has always been true. It's only in our confusion that we view this healthy movement as a general rebelliousness. But an act of self-responsibility and self-discipline is not the same as an act of childish self-will that refutes genuine authority.

Inwardly, though, when we assume responsibility for ourselves, we may rebel against the short-term uncertainty of stepping into what seems like a vacuum, created after we give up our tight self-will and start to let go. We'd rather trust our own false gods—namely, our ego—than trust the process of letting go.

In our relationships with other people, we can observe how our forcing current exerts a subtle pressure saying, "You have to love me." Sadly, this creates anything but love. Perhaps we feel it would be impossible to give up our demand because we can't stand the idea of not being loved. Aren't we entitled to getting some love? Isn't this benign universe supposed to give it to us? How can we possibly give up our demand and be content with the bleak emptiness we fear will follow?

These are good questions. But they don't change the truth that the attitude that says 'you must' draws everything else but love to our doorstep. It's just a fact that a closed energy system sprouting out of distrust, non-love, power-drives and half-truths cannot breed love. Perhaps we can sense this tightness in ourselves, this holding on out of fear. Our unwillingness to let go always points to an inner struggle about knowing what to trust: God or our little ego.

If we want to learn to trust God, we will need to travel through some interim self-created states of mind. But as so often happens, we are hoping we can avoid what we ourselves have created, including pain, confusion, emptiness and fear. Nonetheless, these are the things we're going to need to embrace so we can come to understand them on our way to dissolving them.

There's a huge difference between thinking a temporary state of reality is the final story—so we should keep it at arms length—and knowing it's only temporary. If we think a condition is final, we'll either resist letting it go or we'll fall into a pit of resignation, believing we'll be unhappy and helpless forever.

That's why we pitch such a fit about letting go. We'd rather keep things the way they are than risk falling into these states of consciousness we created and through which we are destined to go before we can let go and create the life we long for. This is our current dilemma, even though letting go and letting God feels wonderful and safe. We just need to give it a try so we can have this experience, and so our resistance to letting go will finally, well, let go. This isn't a one-time event. We have to make this decision to let go over and over.

If we notice a certain tightness in ourselves at this suggestion, we can likely trace it to a current that says, "But I want it so bad." Our desperation, though, is not caused by not having what we want—it is due to the tightness that is shutting God out. Our contracted state of tightness comes from a concept of poverty that justifies our belief that we need to grasp and hold on.

We mistakenly think that giving up our tight self-will means giving up our wish. It really means giving up the insistence of our wish. So the wish must be let loose *temporarily*, which is totally different from giving it up altogether. We need to momentarily give up the 'who, what, where, when and how' of the thing we want. Once we've let it go, we may be able to come back to the same 'who, what, where, when and how,' but the wish can then manifest in a completely different climate.

Often the thing that limits our wish fulfillment is our insistence that fulfillment can only come in one specific way. But if we let the creative process have some rope and margin, we'll experience that it by far surpasses what we hoped for or could visualize. Our ego mind can hardly conceive of the richness of the universe. We need to learn to empty ourselves in the moment so the divine can reveal itself to us. This is what it means to "let God."

Another thing we may need to let go of is our negative image of our life in which we think we can only suffer. A hidden belief such as this must be examined and ousted so we can inactivate its energetic power to create. This can't happen if we're holding on in a fighting spirit against such a negative belief.

It's the same if we're sending out currents of domination over those we love, fighting against their imperfections and immaturities that cause us pain. We do so because we don't trust that our inner God—our Higher Self with its divine aspects and connection—can produce fulfillment for us unless we rule over others, imposing our ideas on them. The issue is not about how right or wrong our ideas are, but about our insisting that others follow them.

This is the conflict humanity finds itself caught in: we either hold on, bracing against the bleakness, hurt feelings and empty existence we fear will be our fate if we let go, or we resign ourselves to such a dismal state so we can not hold on. Welcome back to the land of duality. It's either a forcing current or resigned acceptance of a miserable state, which of course makes us hopeless and causes us to harbor a belief that life is fundamentally cruel. Seldom does this conflict apply to every area of our life, but almost always we can see where it applies to some.

Outwardly, we may lean more towards one of these attitudes, but we can then be sure the other lies hiding in the wings. So if, for example, we are outwardly very aggressive and forceful, we may tend to get our way through sheer force, cleverly manipulating people or possibly persuading using dishonesty. If this is the case—perhaps only in certain areas—we're using some of our energy to cover up our despair and resignation, our distrust of life.

Conversely, we might be the type who, more than anything, wants to get along with others; we depend on them and don't want to antagonize them. Beneath this must be a desire to dominate, which we might enact through submission: "I'll be happy to do whatever you say, so then you'll be bound to me and have to obey me. I'll make sure you feel too guilty to offend me, after I've proven how obedient I am to you." Such hidden attitudes must be found and explored.

Once we become aware of one attitude manifesting outwardly, we must not be deluded into thinking the opposite doesn't exist in us. If we're outwardly dominant, it may be harder to find the inner hopelessness. If we're outwardly weak, dependent and submissive, we may struggle in dealing with our covert manipulation. Two sides, one coin.

If our chosen strategy seems to work—we seem to get our way—it will be harder to see all that we miss. But eventually, life is going to bring home the truth that our succeeding is an illusion. We're fighting a state of emptiness that only exists because of our chosen solution. If we see this, perhaps it will motivate us to stop chasing our tail and start dealing with this struggle.

The problem with all of our defensive strategies is that momentarily they may work. But in the long run, they don't give us what we're really yearning for: real fulfillment. The very use of the pseudo-solution of aggression or submission—or perhaps withdrawal into false serenity, if nothing else works—makes this impossible.

Let's say, for instance, that we want love and closeness with another person. But we're certain we won't get this if things are left to the others free will. Let's further suppose we like to rule by demanding and coercing, using jealousy, domination and possessiveness. Keep in mind, we can come at this from either side, overtly or covertly, ruling by dependency and blaming and making the other feel guilty as an option.

If the other partially truly loves us, but also partially needs us neurotically, they will submit to our rule. But they are going to also resent us and blame us and defy us—even though they have their own skin in the game and are party to this arrangement. So yay, we succeeded. But what did we get? It won't fill our real need for closeness as we will constantly be battling those reactions that we are half-responsible for. Worst of all, the negative reactions from the other will validate our hidden belief that 'see, I knew it's

Letting Go & Letting God

a cruel world and I can never be happy.' Third verse, same as the first.

But what would happen if we let go of the reins? What if we had the courage and integrity to let go, notwithstanding our fear that our partner would leave? If we lose, what have we lost? But if we win, imagine the joy of finding out the other wants to love us freely, without needing to be dominated, coerced or manipulated. That's the true richness we've been looking for.

And what if we were to lose this person—does this mean we must be alone forever? Of course not. But temporarily, we may have to dip into the bleakness so we can dissolve the power it has to obstruct us. In doing so, we "let God."

Make a note of this: divine creation wants nothing but the best for us. If we can confront our doubt that this is true, we can start to establish trust. We can come to have faith in the abundance of life by looking at where we won't let go and let God because that seems to connote resignation to an unfulfilled life. We can sense the shift in our inner being when we stop grabbing; we can then visualize ourselves in a patient, humble state of mind, confident that the universe will give us its best.

Abundance is floating around us constantly, but our clogged energy systems and defensive strategies create walls that close us off from it. In a closed energy system, we see ourselves as paupers and don't avail ourselves of our own wealth. Whether we want a relationship, a specific job, friends, people who will buy what we're selling or receive what we're giving or give us what we're looking for, we need to live in an open energy system. We must be willing to reach out into life and claim its riches.

To be energetically compatible with the riches of the universe, we have to be rich ourselves. Being rich implies we're generous, humble and honest enough to not exert force over others. If we're rich, we don't need to force, because forcing really amounts to stealing and we know there's no reason to force when what we desire will be freely given to us. Here's the grand irony: what the universe wants to give us freely becomes inaccessible when we force.

By the same token, when we won't let go, we violate our own sense of integrity. Deep down, this makes us doubt ourselves and our right to be happy. To not let go then is like being a beggar, grasping at straws in an effort to be happy. But if we're willing to let go, we can establish the fact of our ultimate richness deep in our psyche. This may mean we need to take a hard look at our illusions and pretenses, and all our little dishonesties. But cleared of these distortions, we will be rich indeed.

The key to creating an open energy system is letting go into trust. But we can't get there is one giant step. We must lay down some intermediate links, without skipping steps along the way. These links will build a bridge to having genuine, positive expectations about life free from pressure, anxiety and doubt. We'll develop a deep faith in a kind and caring universe where we can have the very best, in every possible way. What a valuable key.

To create the open energy system needed for richness to flow into us—from outside ourselves and surfacing from within—we need to have a richness that can afford to lose in the moment. Then we'll be able to tolerate the short-lived pain of finding out what really blocks our fulfillment; we'll have the patience to remove the obstruction by changing a faulty inner attitude. That's the path to building richness from our poverty.

Here are the steps we must take. Step One: find where we struggle between pushing and applying pressure, and falling into hopelessness. Step Two: realize that this conflict exists because we're convinced we're poor and can't have what we want without forcing and holding on. Step Three: commit to finding out the real reason for our nonfulfillment by surfacing misconceptions about life, unearthing our negative intention towards life, feeling the pain of not having our desires met and our belief that it will always be so. This will require honesty, patience and perseverance in working with someone who can help us see our hidden distortions. Plus we'll need to have the humility to not blame others or the universe for our own poverty, but instead search our own soul for where it lives inside us.

We all feel rich in some areas and poor in others. Maybe we're rich in the area of creative talents—its like a stream that never ceases to flow—but we feel poor about ever finding true mutuality in a relationship. Another may feel secure in that area, but doubt they can ever have financial security. We need to get clear about which we experience where.

Where we are rich, we will always be rich because we have an open, giving and honest attitude. But where we're poor, we'll be poor until we see what we've been blind to. What does it look like when we believe we are poor? Wherever we are pushing, domineering and manipulating, we are essentially cheating. When put into words, our behavior is basically saying, "I will force you to give me what you won't freely give me. If power doesn't work, I'll use trickery. I'll make you feel guilty for not giving me what I want, and will blame you for making me a victim. I'll accuse you of doing what I am secretly doing." It would take a miracle to find any love in that. This is an unfair, cheating attitude that totally attempts to stomp on the freedom of the other person. The energetic form of it is a tight prison or a short leash.

On the other hand, an open energy system would sound more like this: "Since I love you, I would be happy to have your love. But I give you the freedom to come to me if and when you choose. If you don't love me, I have no right to make you feel guilty by pretending that I am devastated by this." There is an honesty, decency and integrity in this that creates richness.

We are entitled to want a loving relationship, or to have financial security or whatever, but going about it the wrong way prohibits fulfillment and is essentially dishonest. Because if we feel poor, we think we must steal. And if we keep stealing, we keep staying poor, for only the honest are deserving of the riches. Stealing leads to guilt and our guilt produces doubt that we are entitled to receive freely. Toot toot, the train's back at the station.

It may help to understand the difference between guilt and shame and remorse. When we feel guilt, we are in effect saying, "I'm beyond redemption and deserve to feel devastated." We feel this way because we believe that our Lower Self is all of us. Our Lower Self is the part characterized by our negativity, immaturity, destructiveness, ignorance, malice, spite, dishonesty and manipulation, which is only a temporary aspect of us, brought here to Earth so we can recognize it and transform it. We need to be aware of this powerful and dangerous wrong thinking. It's not true and it's an insult to God and all of creation, of which we—including our Higher Self—are an integral part.

Our self-devastating guilt is also integrally linked with our distrust of life. Our guilt causes us to cut ourselves off from the flow of divinity by going immediately to whitewashing our faults and failings—which of course are the areas we need to be facing and honestly owning. Going over to this opposite extreme is a defense against acknowledging our shortcomings for which we feel such self-devastating guilt. It reveals a denial of the true nature of life—a lack of trust in an all-loving, all-giving universe open to all created beings. It's not a constructive attitude, nor is it realistic, and it won't lead us anywhere good on our path of self-purification. We must deal with our double-edged distortion around guilt and set it right.

How about shame? Shame is an emotion connected to vanity and appearance. We might be ashamed to let others see some aspect of ourselves because we like to pretend we are better than we are. The ego's ideal version of the self is more important than what's real and true. So we lose contact with the treasure of our real self. Whereas guilt relates to how we feel about our inner self—we're playing a game about how devastated we are about it and we exaggerate it—shame is about our image in other people's eyes; we're putting up a pretense about who we really are and don't want to be seen in truth.

True remorse has nothing to do with either of these. With remorse, we are simply recognizing where we fall short—our faults and impurities, our shortcomings and limitations—admitting that there are parts of us that violate spiritual law. We feel regret and are willing to admit the truth about our destructiveness, recognizing that it's a useless waste of energy and hurts others and ourselves. We sincerely want to change. With remorse, our self-confrontation is completely different from self-devastating guilt or shame.

If we feel remorseful, it is possible to say, "It's true that I have this or that shortcoming or fault—I'm petty or dishonest, I have false pride or hatred or whatever—but this isn't all of who I am. The part of me that recognizes, regrets and wants to change is aligned with my divine self—my Higher Self—which ultimately will overcome whatever I feel remorseful about." In this case, the "I" that can dislike aspects of ourselves and wants to change those destructive, untruthful, deviating aspects doesn't fall apart, even as it notices that something needs to be healed.

Guilt involves a lack of faith in All That Is, while shame is all about appearances and it will lift off the more we risk exposing our defects and aligning with the truth of who we really are. Remorse is an emotion that will carry us home, feeling the sadness of the effects of our Lower Self and motivating us to discover the true source of all life, which is what we can find when we let go and let God.

#213 The Spiritual and the Practical Meaning of "Let Go, Let God"

PEARLS

About the Author

A neatnik with a ready sense of humor, Jill Loree's first job as a root-beer-stand carhop in Northern Wisconsin was an early sign that things could only get better.

She would go on to throw pizzas and bartend while in college, before discovering that the sweet spot of her 30-year sales-and-marketing career would be in business-to-business advertising. A true Gemini with a degree in Chemistry and a flair for writing, she enjoys the challenge of thinking creatively about scientific topics. Her brain fires on both the left and right sides.

That said, her real passion in life has been her spiritual path. Raised in the Lutheran faith, she became a more deeply spiritual person in the rooms of AA, a spiritual recovery program, starting in 1989. In 1997, she was introduced to the wisdom of the Pathwork, which she describes as "having walked through the doorway of a fourth step and found the whole library."

She completed four years of Pathwork Helpership training in 2007 followed by four years of apprenticing and discernment before stepping into her full Helpership in 2011. She has been a teacher in the Transformation Program offered at Sevenoaks Retreat Center in Madison, Virginia, operated by Mid-Atlantic Pathwork, where she also led marketing activities for over two years and served on the Board of Trustees.

In 2012, Jill completed four years of Kabbalah training in a course called the Soul's Journey, achieving certification for hands-on healing using the energies embodied in the tree of life.

Not bad for a former pom-pom squad captain who once played Dolly in *Hello Dolly!* She is now the proud mom to two adult children, Charlie and Jackson, who were born and raised in Atlanta. Having grown weary of borrowing other people's last names, Jill now happily uses her middle name as her last—it's pronounced la-REE. In her spare time, she enjoys reading, writing, running, yoga and hiking, especially in the mountains.

As she turns the corner onto the back nine in life, she has consciously decoupled from the corporate world and is now dedicating her life to writing and spiritual teaching.

Discover more from Jill Loree at www.phoenesse.com.

More from Jill Loree

Real. Clear.
A Seven-Book Series of Spiritual Teachings

The *Real. Clear.* series offers a fresh approach to timeless spiritual teachings by way of easier-to-read language; it's the Guide's wisdom in Jill Loree's words. Each book is written with a bit of levity because, as Mary Poppins put it, "A spoonful of sugar helps the medicine go down."

HOLY MOLY: The Story of Duality, Darkness and Daring Rescue

There's one story, as ancient and ageless as anything one can imagine, that lays a foundation on which all other truths stand. It exposes the origin of opposites. It illuminates the reality of darkness in our midst. It speaks of herculean efforts made on our behalf. This is that story.

FINDING GOLD: The Search for Our Own Precious Self

The journey to finding the whole amazing nugget of the true self is a lot like prospecting for gold. Both combine the lure of potential and the excitement of seeing a sparkling possibility, with needing to have the patience of a saint.

It helps to have a map of our inner landscape and a headlamp for seeing into dark corners. That's what Jill Loree has created in this collection of spiritual teachings called *Finding Gold*.

BIBLE ME THIS: Releasing the Riddles of Holy Scripture

The Bible is a stumper for many of us, not unlike the Riddler teasing Batman with his "Riddle me this" taunts. But what if we could know what some of those obscure passages mean? What's the truth hidden in the myth of Adam & Eve? And what was up with that Tower of Babel?

Bible Me This is a collection of in-depth answers to a variety of questions asked of the Guide about the Bible.

THE PULL: Relationships & their Spiritual Significance

The Pull is about discovering the truth about relationships: they are the doorway through which we ultimately can come to know ourselves, God and another person; through them, we can learn to fully live. Because while life may be many things, more than anything else, it is all about relationships.

The Pull walks us through the delicate dance of intimate relationships, helping us navigate one of the most challenging aspects of life.

PEARLS: A Mind-Opening Collection of 17 Fresh Spiritual Teachings

In this classic, practical collection, Jill Loree strings together timeless spiritual teachings, each carefully polished with a light touch. Topics include: Privacy & Secrecy • The Lord's Prayer • Political Systems • The Superstition of Pessimism • Preparing to Reincarnate • Our Relationship to Time • Grace & Deficit • The Power of Words • Perfectionism • Authority • Order • Positive Thinking • Three Faces of Evil • Meditation for Three Voices • The Spiritual Meaning of Crisis • Leadership • Letting Go & Letting God

GEMS: A Multifaceted Collection of 16 Clear Spiritual Teachings

Clear and radiant, colorful and deep, each sparkling gem in this collection of spiritual teachings taken mostly from the final 50 lectures out of nearly 250, offers a ray of light to help illuminate our steps to reaching Oneness.

BONES: A Building-Block Collection of 19 Fundamental Spiritual Teachings

This collection is like the bones of a body—a framework around which the remaining body of work can arrange itself. Sure, there's a lot that needs to be filled in to make it all come to life, but with *Bones*, now we've got the basic building blocks in place. Plus the words go down like a strawberry milkshake—pleasing to the tongue yet with all the calcium we need for optimum health.

Self. Help.
A Two-Book Teaching Series

The *Self. Help.* series offers a bird's-eye view of the Guide's teachings and how to apply them in working with others.

SPILLING THE SCRIPT: An Intense Guide to Self-Knowing

Now, for the first time, powerful spiritual teachings from the Guide are available in one concise book. Jill Loree has written *Spilling the Script* to deliver a clear, high-level perspective about self-discovery and healing, giving us the map we need for following this life-changing path to Oneness.

The goal of this spiritual journey is to make contact with our divine core so we can transition from living in duality to discovering the joy of being in unity. For even as we believe ourselves to be victims of an unfair universe, the truth is that we are continually guarding ourselves against pain, and through our defended approach to life we unknowingly bring about our current life circumstances. But we can make new choices

Bit by bit, as we come out of the trance we have been in, we begin to see cause and effect, and to take responsibility for the state of our lives. Gradually, our lives transform. We once again can sense our essential nature and eternal connectedness with all that is.

In the course of this work, we develop on various levels of our being. In our spirit, we move from the separation of duality to unity. In our mind, we move from wrong conclusions to truth. In our will, we move from forcing currents and withholding to receptivity and a willingness to give. In our emotions, we move from being blocked and numb to being loving and flexible. In our bodies, we move from being frozen and split to being open and integrated.

Over time, we will develop discernment and a truer perception about the world around us. We will shift from our defensiveness, to a stance of openness and transparency. We will be wise in our self-disclosure and rigorous in self-honesty. We will learn to become vulnerable and we will know peace.

"You will find how you cause all your difficulties. You have already stopped regarding these words as mere theory, but the better you progress, the more will you truly understand just how and why you cause your hardships. By so doing, you gain the key to changing your life."
– Pathwork Guide, Lecture #78

HEALING THE HURT: How to Heal Using Spiritual Guidance

The work of healing our fractured inner selves takes a little finesse, a lot of stick-to-it-iveness, and the skilled help of someone who has gone down this road before. Being a Helper then is about applying all we have learned on our own healing journey to help guide others through the process of reunifying their fragmented hidden places.

That may sound simple, but it's surely not easy. It's also not easy to be the Worker, the one who does this work of spiritual healing. Now, with *Healing the Hurt*, everyone can understand the important skills needed by a Helper to assure Workers find what they're looking for.

Pithy Cakes
Quippy Confections About
Making it Through

Pithy Cakes is a collection of a few dozen original confections, mash-ups of Jill Loree's life and spiritual path. Crafted to edify and also delight, they are short, a bit fun, and made to hit the spot. Sort of like a cupcake. The frosting? A handful of poems sprinkled about.

Made with inspiration. Best enjoyed with coffee.

The Guide Speaks
The Complete Q&A Collection
By Eva Pierrakos
with Jill Loree

www.theguidespeaks.org

In *The Guide Speaks*, Jill Loree opens up this fascinating collection of thousands of Q&As from the Pathwork Guide, all arranged alphabetically by topic. The website, www.theguidespeaks.org, includes hard-hitting questions asked and answered about religion, Jesus Christ, the Bible, reincarnation, the Spirit World, death, prayer and meditation, God and so much more.

"There are so many questions you need to ask, personal and general ones. In the end they become one and the same. The lectures I am called upon to deliver are also answers to unspoken questions, questions that arise out of your inner yearning, searching, and desires to know and to be in truth. They arise out of your willingness to find divine reality, whether this attitude exists on the conscious or unconscious level.

But there are other questions that need to be asked deliberately on the active, outer, conscious level in order to fulfill the law. For only when you knock can the door be opened; only when you ask can you be given. This is a law."

– The Pathwork Guide in Q&A #250

Made in the USA
Middletown, DE
28 July 2016